# Paris
## on a plate

STEPHEN DOWNES

# Paris on a plate

## A gastronomic diary

PIER **9**

# contents

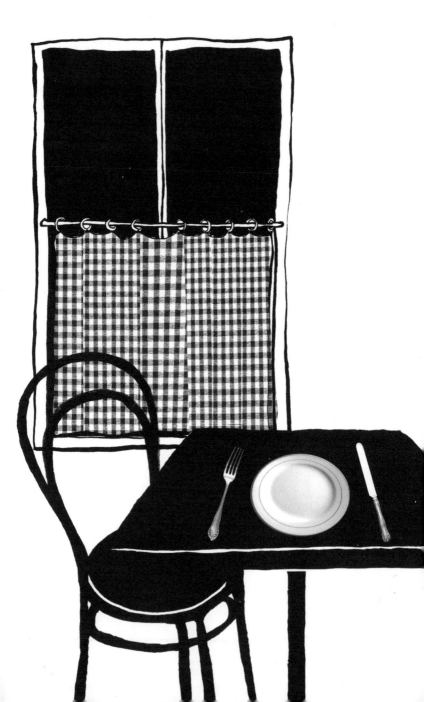

# prologue

If man were meant to hover, he would be doing it with less fuss. All of us inside the belly of our Hovercraft — that brilliant British invention — thought so as we shuddered towards France. Even the English.

I'd been watching them from a disrespectful distance for months. An Australian simpleton, I felt they were odd. In fact, the Hovercraft was an embodiment of everything British — classically mad. Clearly, crazily idiotic. Small, the idea worked: hovercrafts were fine as lawnmowers and turf dryers. But, being English, the English had extrapolated the idea to absurd dimensions. A hovercraft would be made to walk on water. They would call its cross-Channel adventures 'flights'. (Mind you, if you'd told an Australian you needed to cross the Channel in a hurry, he'd probably have said, 'You got two arms? Start swimming!') Any fool could have told the English an enormous hovercraft wouldn't work. A real European — from east of Calais — could not have thought up *the* Hovercraft. And if he had, he'd have got out of bed, wiped his brow, thrown down a tranquillising cognac and returned to his lover.

The English could be 'different'; lesson number one. In less than a year I'd learnt to pick a man wearing socks under his sandals from two hundred metres. Or a woman wearing a small animal around her neck. For warmth? Or companionship? It was a handy talent to have on London transport. You developed the skill of avoiding passengers who had urgent news for you. Some reported humans on Neptune. Others prattled strange sayings into their knees and looked at you sideways.

But now I was trapped, hovering across the Channel on a day that was clear and sunny somewhere else. I could see through murky windows as far as the next wave. Beyond that, a grey curtain fell over life. The sea was the colour of pale jade and as spiky as a waxed hairdo. Spray spattered the windows with the tireless rhythms of a porno stud. The Hovercraft shuddered and juddered, bellowed, leapt and lunged.

And filled with smoke, although we weren't sinking. The further they got from England, the more the Brits smoked. They were, after all, about to confront 'foreigners', who began at Calais. Or even Boulogne, where we were going. It was a marginal day for hovercrafting, the crew had warned us. 'Not the Serpentine,' smiled a purser in a shirt redolent of light work.

All of this was of secondary importance to me, of course. I was excited by more cerebral things. Recently twenty-five, I'd quit Australia ten months earlier with no plans to go back. I'd lapsed badly from a strict Methodist upbringing in the process. I'd betrayed both church and country by enjoying life. To the extreme. Energetically, in fact. It was 1971, after all. And now I was off to Paris for the first time, which, for an antipodean Protestant, was as naughty as you could get. It had severely thrilling potential. It was a world-heritage-listed site of sin, I understood. Devoted to hedonism. The French were Catholic, Methodism had taught us. Immoral, they sinned, and then scurried to confession. They went to dirty movies — *made* them — and drank red wine instead of weak tea with meals. But Paris was also supposed to be the world's most beautiful city. This was handy. It provided a legitimate reason to visit.

Clifford and Moira from Southend sat next to me. They were about to visit Boulogne for the day with as much enthusiasm as a male attending prenatal classes. They'd wanted to go to Spain, said Moira, a big woman in a dress of printed jonquils. Have a proper holiday. But France was all they could afford. They'd buy some red meat, she rationalised. Perhaps a nice leg of lamb.

Clifford was wearing shorts, for three reasons, no doubt: he was English, it was April, and he was having a day off. His sensible sandals had thin leather soles and wide brass buckles. They were strapped to feet hosed in red woollen socks with *fleur de lys* above the heels. His bare legs were whiter than a corpse. He peered grimly through dirty lenses at the spatterings of spray. Two veils over the world. And he smoked more than anyone else, drawing in enough fumes to fill the Albert Hall. He exhaled with power and wheeze. I suspected he himself would hover if placed downwards. Moira and he loved a day out, he coughed, before heading off for more waxed bags. She'd filled three already. She held them tight across her bosom as if they were presents for her grandchildren. If she stood up she'd feel worse, she said. Clifford had his hands full just getting up the aisle. He clamped his cigarette in his mouth to hang on better.

The Poms and I had declared an uneasy truce. I could live with them if I had to. But only just. Since arriving in London I'd irritated them by doing all the usual expat-ocker things. I'd been employed and sacked in a matter of weeks. (I'd contracted glandular fever, and you couldn't keep on someone who'd caught 'the kissing disease', the argument must have gone at the *Sunday Express*. Not that they'd let me in on it.) I'd fought an Indian landlord's bath times and cooking odours. I'd moved to Earl's Court. I'd aged in dole queues and acquired almost-free spectacles. I'd had blood drawn by an African and my arse caressed by an editor. I'd done my time. If I liked Europe enough to want to cross over, then I owed the English nothing. Whimsy was legitimate. I was free!

I was confident of finding work anywhere. And if I couldn't, I was the kind of person who could live off frozen vegetables and cheap mince. I bought them by the ounce. I was hermetically sealed against accidents, illness and malnutrition, impossibly secure. I also had thick socks and a warm jacket. I could settle wherever there was a bed and a pillow. They didn't even have to be comfy. I didn't need space, either. Apart from clothes and a pair of zip-up boots, I owned a foot's length of books, a tartan rug and a portable typewriter. I could dance around Europe as easily, say, as Ali around a ring.

And there was something about this France place that intrigued me. It might be beautiful, and it might be full of Catholic filth, but it was also supposed to have class. I held to a ridiculous vision of a whole nation of smart people. Discerning, too. They could pick quality from rubbish. Photographs showed them in tailored suits that were freshly pressed and worn to the millimetre. *And* they ate well — everyone knew that. The best, in fact. Even Methodists knew no nation ate better. They sniffed their red wine and could tell if it was good or vinegar. Their novelists wrote fat books that were supposed to be very perceptive about the human condition. And, I thought, this immature Australian thought, I'd love to try to match it with this mob. Not just see what makes them tick, see if they really do have it all, but challenge them to improve my lot. 'Enrich me, Froggies!' I'd demand.

The Hovercraft staggered from the sea, exhausted, settling with relief onto its concrete landing pad. It farted thunderous sprays. Its engines screamed a last pained crescendo — it hadn't wanted to be a Hovercraft — then fell silent. We were as done in as the beast. Bedraggled and ill, the heart and soul of British tourism staggered along a cement walkway to a customs hall.

If this was France, then nothing had changed. More buildings constructed for a purpose, not an aesthetic. Well, perhaps a few things were different: in plain block letters we were urged to *NE PAS FUMER* and *FAITES LA QUEUE.* Make the queue? To where? For what? Beyond the signs, unmanned cream counters bordered an empty space. A poster on the wall displayed an angry-looking lobster about to attack. Its caption claimed something about Brittany's seafood.

We made our queue and waited. Moira recovered some colour, and she and Clifford were led off to an anteroom to be processed for Boulogne. The rest of us were bound for Paris. We understood this when a band of railwaymen set upon us. They were convincing. Identically serious in hue and manner, they wore white shirts and thin dark ties knotted tightly at the neck. Over these were grey, V-necked pullovers and close-fitting jackets in a midnight shade. Peaked caps, grey trousers and peremptory manners completed their ensembles. On their breasts the logo of the French railways, SNCF, scintillated in gold. Each had a black calfskin book — the Book of Railway, no doubt — under an official armpit.

As a group, they began waving broadly with their free hands, shouting '*Paris! Paris!*' When shouting failed to move us, they began herding. Ahead of their flapping arms, we shuffled forward through heavy glass doors towards a platform. It was getting dark. The railwaymen shouted louder, '*Paris par là! Là! Là!*'

We spread along the platform. Facing us was an untidy embankment, sparsely vegetated with weeds. They looked dry, as weeds do in Australia, not green like English weeds. As in prisoner-of-war movies, we straggled into a thin, tired trickle.

A train would arrive soon, the SNCF herders made us understand. But we must *not* get on it. It was not a train for us, not *our* train. Our train was another train, they scowled, taking up strategic positions along the platform. They seemed to be daring us to board any train at all.

Dun-green carriages stuttered to a halt, drawn by a hissing locomotive. We made for the doors. '*Non!*' shouted the SNCF men in unison. '*Non!*' This was not *our* train. But it *was* Agincourt again. England versus France, the tourists pressing forward, the SNCF men resisting. Spreading their arms, the French attempted a series of pincer movements.

'They always reckon it's never this train,' said an Irish accent next to me. 'Just push on board. All the trains go to Paris.' The voice belonged to a crumpled man who obviously travelled a lot. He looked as if it was his job. He carried a bulging canvas sausage bag. Protruding from a voluminous khaki raincoat was a dark, epic face. His hair was messy. He might have been wrapped for throwing out.

'You know the ropes,' I said in a congratulatory tone.

'Know the Froggies,' he affirmed. 'Just push.'

We did. An SNCF man caught me. He was affronted. '*Paris?*' he clipped. Yes, I said, waving my Hovercraft-Train-All-In-One-Eleven-Pound-Return ticket at him. He glanced at it, then pulled the Book of Railway from under his arm. 'This is not *your* train,' he read appositely from its pages. His words were clear, his accent heavy. 'You have a *special* train for Paris.'

'Just get in,' shouted the Irishman, who was disappearing ahead.

'All trains from here go to Paris,' I ventured, smug in my new knowledge. I swept an arm down the track, hoping Paris was that way.

'Perhaps that is so,' said the SNCF man. 'But you don't go in this train.'

'Why not?' I persevered.

'Because it is not *your* train,' he pronounced.

'But, if it goes to Paris, it's all the same... For me.'

'But it is not *your* train,' he protested firmly, waving his bible.

I could sense the tightness of his tie. A gale force of garlic breath engulfed me. It possessed a special meaning, something profound. Would this railwayman really want to herd cantankerous British tourists around his station while his dinner was getting cold? I didn't think so. I played what I hoped was a trump.

'*Paris est Paris,*' I said with a smile, following up even more daringly — and in an atrocious accent — with, '*et un train est un train.*'

Paris was Paris and a train was a train for him, too, apparently. And philosophy was *philo*, something French children studied at school. He smiled knowingly. Cartesian to his comfortable black lace-ups, he was clearly overwhelmed by my impressive logic. He opened his bible, looked one last time, then closed it and dropped his hands to his sides.

'*Allez-y, monsieur,*' he said, gesturing me on board.

I scrambled for a window seat. If all the French were like him they would be easy to like. These people took it on the chin, didn't obfuscate or doublespeak. They didn't want to argue. Logic was more important. They said what they thought and clearly appreciated others who did the same.

Hovercraft veterans poured in after me. Through the windows, I watched the not so valiant — the more English, perhaps, or at least the more polite — trying to be less forthright. The French overwhelmed them.

A few minutes later, the train clanked away from the platform, gathering speed to a reluctant, if brisk, walking pace. Within a hundred metres we passed through a cutting. Its crusty geological face was scattered with dull, scrubby plants and dried grass a metre tall. I hadn't seen vegetation so distressed since leaving worn old Australia. Instantly, weirdly and without reason, I felt strangely at home. At home in

France! The idea astonished me: it was absurd. This was a foreign land. I couldn't believe it wasn't. But perhaps in some ways it was like home. Perhaps, I would like it. Even like it a lot, I thought, as night fell.

A friend in London — a well-travelled Englishman of no few years — had jotted down an important address for me. 'Keep it in your wallet at all times,' he'd advised. It was an office in Paris that found people rooms. 'Open most hours,' he'd added, 'just in case'. I juggled the phone and my wallet and pulled out a tiny slip of paper. '*BUREAU D'ACCUEIL*,' he'd written, followed by Paris's best address, the Champs Elysées.

   With not much effort on its part, the vinyl suitcase and I struggled out of the Gare du Nord into a black night that had put on garlands of lights. So many of them. Overdressed? The jury would stay out. But, gee, Paris scintillated. I found a taxi and showed its 'chauffeur' — as I understood you called them, even if there wasn't glass between you — my slip of paper. We accelerated away.

   For every first-time visitor to a country that uses another tongue, there comes a moment when the language must be tried not in stammering ripostes but to start a conversation. As we turned into the Champs Elysées (which I had recognised without difficulty — the lights, again) my moment of Gallic truth arrived.

   'Champs Elysées,' I pronounced with worn awe.

   '*Mais oui*,' said the chauffeur wistfully, lightly tapping his steering wheel. '*Les* Champs Elysées.'

   A fair fraction of the world's peoples were in Paris that night. Most of them were without hotel rooms. Moreover, they were all counting on the Bureau d'Accueil. I 'made' another queue, half-an-hour passing before it was my turn. A small and unsmiling brunette manned the counter. She had centuries of pragmatism bred into her — a gene predisposed to it — and a cool respect for diplomacy. In which part of Paris would I like my hotel, she demanded brusquely in fair English. I had no idea. Then, what number of stars would I like my hotel to possess? Hmmm. None showing through the roof, I countered. She frowned, her brown eyes narrowing under a prim fringe. She peered over her counter at my suitcase.

'Two is good for you,' she said.

'Absolutely,' I agreed, having no idea what two, three, four or even twenty-six stars would entitle me to in terms of pillow softness.

'Two is for students and less,' she said. 'Now you will live in the Latin *Quartier*. It is where all the young people are.' She made a phone call, babbling quickly, and scribbled the hotel's name and address on an official-looking docket. I was to go to the Hotel Pierwige. I begged her pardon.

'Pierwige!' she stressed. The name sounded like someone coughing through fudge. It was on the boulevard Saint-Germain. I would enjoy it. She directed me to get another taxi and have a good stay in Paris. Peering through her fringe, she beckoned the next refo.

Another chauffeur to impress. I passed him the Pierwige's details and we were off. At speed, as usual. The cab smelt of fresh plastic and old cigarettes. I wound down the windows, letting in Paris's own peculiar smell. I already knew London's odour: a blend of stale humans and perished rubber. And I knew Singapore's, which was raw sewerage and five-spice. (New York, I would later decide, smelt of wet steel and raincoats.) I sniffed the air. Paris's odour was up-market biscuits. Something sweet, but a complex flavour, too. A perfume you could chew.

The city of lights truly had them in diamonds. They hung in catenaries or emphasised commerce in discreet bright signs. Cars, vans and motorcycles, all moving briskly, seemed to be pumping life itself through the avenues. They were the city's blood. Traffic was even called '*la circulation*'. I expected more tooting of klaxons, though. There was merely a low hum; Paris repressed aural distractions. Like a stripper without her music, it would seduce you by looks alone, in style and silence. Occasionally, the city's expectant bass line was interrupted by cobblestones, the taxi's suspension parlaying urgent and sensuous harmonics, a mellifluous brrrrrrrr. We alternated between wide boulevards bordered by lights and narrow dimmer streets, cliffs of buildings on either side. On the tight footpaths I glimpsed the most elegant heels I had ever seen.

The taxi stopped near a corner. '*C'est là, monsieur*,' said the chauffeur. Indeed, the Hotel Pierwige certainly was. A modest sign hanging vertically above a second-floor balcony announced its name, the letters backlit in a kind of schoolboy modernist font. I wrestled the case through the hotel's narrow front door.

The reception was cupboard-sized. To the left was an alcove, a partitioned box for keys hanging on the wall behind it. To the right was a door bearing the strict capitals '*SALLE A MANGER*'. Two steps ahead, a wooden staircase began a tight spiral, disappearing heavenwards. A large woman in a floral apron and erratically smudged scarlet lips appeared from a door behind it.

'*Monsieur?*' she enquired. I showed her my docket. She took it, scowled and brushed past me into the alcove with a stern '*Excusez-moi*'. She swung a hinged counter down in front of her and demanded my passport. She looked at it, then me, several times before pencilling my details into her log. The sevens of Australian citizen number 3870721 were crossed with certainty. Within seconds, I was taped. Was I booking in for life? She jabbed an index finger at the steep staircase, informing me to ascend to the '*cinquième étage*'.

The suitcase and I began a definitive bout. I couldn't believe that craftsmen still lived who could hew such tightly curled banisters. Each floor had a landing the size of a Muslim prayer mat, three doors opening off it. Many seemed curiously ajar, and from behind some escaped fragments of French. Beyond a half-open door on the fourth floor, two girls lounged on a ruffled bedspread printed with hibiscus. A cloud of sweet smoke hovered above them. They were about twenty; dark, with large eyes. One of them leavened her brunette locks with blonde streaks. She wore what used to be called a negligée — possibly because anyone who appeared in one was clearly negligent when it came to getting dressed. Her hair in a short bob, the other girl had on jeans and a well-balconied bra. Their feet were bare. Without expression, they watched me struggle with the case. I smiled and pushed on to the summit.

My room was small, with a bouncy mattress on an iron frame, a basin in the corner, a narrow window, a single light, and busy wallpaper of indigo daisies. In places, the paper had peeled, then been ripped off. Of honey-coloured hardwood plinths, the floor appeared clean. It shone energetically. A rug the size of a large handkerchief was beside the bed. I swung open the window and threw back its shutters. Paris's expectant counterpoint invaded the room. I smelt biscuit and heard the distant braying of police vehicles. Hungry, I couldn't wait to eat, and within minutes I'd dumped the case and spun back down the stairs.

Across the boulevard, an awning of maroon canvas bore the words 'La Petite Marmite'. At small round tables on the footpath, groups of animated drinkers talked and laughed. Waiters brought them beer and tall glasses containing a finger or two of a golden liquid. When they blended it with water, as they all did, it turned milky. I hadn't seen liquids change colour since high-school chemistry classes. So magic, too, was part of eating and drinking in France!

A waiter in a long white apron told me to sit inside, by the window. My table was covered with butcher's paper. Cheap and odd, I thought. A menu was thrust into my hand in seconds. An etiolated basket pressed from thin metal appeared. It contained thick slices of wrist-thin bread. Large holes riddled the bread, and its crust, no doubt, once crackled to the touch. I tried it. If this was the famous baguette, then it was stale.

The list translated easily. Eggs with mayonnaise, house terrine, herring fillets, roast chicken and '*bifteck pommes frites*'. A guidebook I'd read incredulously claimed that steak-and-chips was the French national dish. A suspicion nestled on my shoulder. The one I'd glimpsed before. Perhaps France and Australia were not so far apart after all. Or were they in friendly competition? My liking for Paris was soaring. Urging even greater *rapprochement* — a word I didn't then know — I wondered how French steak-and-chips could possibly be similar to ours. It couldn't be! After all, in bush towns this gastronomic delight amounted to a thin cross-section of rib cut with a bandsaw. It arrived under a smother of gluey mushroom gravy that tasted of starch. Accompanying chips were always more tanned than a stockman's face, but a great deal limper than his penis on pay night.

What did I desire? The waiter stood over me. I fumbled with the menu before stammering, '*Bifteck frites.*'

'Steak and chips,' he affirmed. '*Du vin?*'

The words slid out sneakily from a starting point somewhere between sinuses and nose cartilage. Surprisingly, I understood them. Wine. I was making phenomenal progress. I returned to the menu. House wines were listed by volume. Presuming the 'quarts' and 'demis' were of litres, I ordered a quarter carafe of red. '*Bien!*' said the waiter, who seemed to be treating me like any other normal human being, in contradiction to stories I had heard.

At the next table, a short and shrivelled man with grey hair and a wry smile wiped his plate clean with bread. Cleaning his plate with bread was one thing, but it surprised me when he ate his mop. Using a fork and spoon, he took salad greens from a medium-sized bowl in front of him, warehousing them on the now-pristine crockery. To the bowl he added salt, pepper, vinegar and oil from various small receptacles on the table. After whisking these together with the spoon, he returned the leaves to the bowl and folded the lot over several times. I smiled at him. His grin spread.

Across the room, a plump Frenchman served himself from a large brownstone ceramic. Fillets of thick brown fish dripping oil slid onto his plate. He spooned out rounds of carrot, arcs of onion and a sprig of thyme. His elegant companion hesitated her knife and fork over two breast-like mounds of mayonnaise. Eggs beneath, I supposed. At a table near the door, a sober-looking business type unbuttoned his jacket and began trimming his camembert with a knife.

My steak and wine materialised. Mustard in a small ceramic pot and another pressed-metal basket, this time holding chips, also arrived. I recognised the cut of beef. Back home we called it 'skirt steak'. It was the lowest form of muscle. My mother minced it for Cornish pasties, which were her only gastronomic flourish (if you could dignify pasties with such a description). She cooked them annually, on account of her forebears, she would say, and then grizzled about the amount of work involved in slicing turnips. Skirt steak was cheap and nasty and I had no idea why a café, even of unknown reputation, would be serving it as the national dish. Surely fillet or porterhouse would leap from a substitutes' bench if rib-eye wasn't available? Then I tasted it. Not only tender for a rough cut, it was also delicious. Moreover, once inside its brown-fried exterior, you came across warm-raw, dark maroon flesh. I loved raw meat.

The chips were crisp, their innards of cloudy, blow-away lightness. And what was it about French potatoes that gave them flavour? Spuds were duds where I came from. As a place, I decided quickly, France had increasing attractions. But if the meal had merit, my wine was ugly — sharp and thin.

Salad greens appeared, and I shook salt and pepper onto them. I picked up the oil and was about to add it when my shrivelled friend gestured. '*Ah, non, monsieur!*' he insisted. His grin had disappeared. His shaking head dictated that I put down the oil.

'*Faites l'espace,*' he said, which was beyond my comprehension. He made a clearing motion with his hand.

I picked up the spoon and began toying with the leaves. He gestured again. I cleared some to one side. He grinned. I pushed all the leaves to the edge of the bowl. He was delighted. I picked up the oil again. His grin disappeared.

'*Ah, non, monsieur! D'abord, le sel et le poivre.*' I must have looked mystified; he picked up his own salt and pepper. I sprinkled seasoning into the bowl. We smiled at one other. I picked up the oil. His hand shot out, hooking my elbow.

'*Pas encore, monsieur!*' I replaced the oil. '*En premier, le vinaigre.*'

*Vinaigre?* Had to be. I picked up the vinegar. My instructor smiled. '*Pas trop!*' He accompanied his insistence with a fingertip and thumb only fractionally apart. Perhaps I shouldn't add too much. I poured and replaced, then picked up the oil.

'*Bien!*' he said.

I poured and stirred. He smiled. I pulled back the leaves over the sauce and tossed them. A fulfilled pedagogue, he held his arms aloft like a heavyweight champion.

How much discovery could I cram into a first night? Particularly about food, in which I thought I could perhaps nurture an interest. After all, I'd always liked eating, even if its scope had been limited.

Options swirled as the carafe emptied and a short black followed. I felt light and worldly, ready to argue with Sartre or take on the lions at any nominated zoo. Paris was exhilarating, foreign as nowhere else I'd been. Yet also weirdly accommodating. The sensation of being at home rushed me again. The French did things I felt comfortable with. Enjoyed, even. Their directness and logicality made sense to a practical and marginally serious person. Their rituals were peculiar and attractive, but also exotic. What a combination! I forgave them immediately for stealing steak-and-chips. Men don't generally quiver, but a certain vibration was disturbing me. France was so different from England, which I had been led to believe was part of Europe. Undeniably itself, France was contrary — like me at times. It had a kind of cultural courage, a determination to do things its own way no matter what.

I did a lap of the Left Bank after dinner, taking in the crowds of elegant pedestrians, the nervous traffic, the urgent Parisian police cars and the increasingly complex smell of biscuit.

Finally, I mounted the stairs for bed. They looked sleepier, but nothing else had changed about the girls on the fourth floor. Their door remained open. They smoked still, the fog above their heads thicker. The cloud smelt sweeter and more herbal, and I returned their polite stares for longer. As I continued for the fifth floor, the bobbed one with the balconied bra, dark and quite pretty, flashed the faintest of smiles. She shrugged her shoulders. Slowly. Deliberately? One of the black satin straps supporting her breasts slid over ivory skin to make a loop by her elbow. The faintest pink crest of aureole rose above a lacy black cup. She smiled a fraction more and pouted like a little girl who's had her doll confiscated. I blushed.

I might have learnt a lot since leaving the Hovercraft. But, in a wholly French sense, I still wasn't Einstein.

# day one

Thirty-four years later, the cars and whitegoods, ships and motorbikes recycled from Hovercraft scrap have long since rusted away. And I touch down forty minutes early at Roissy Charles de Gaulle — or Charles de Gaulle Roissy, if you admire the big general more than the airport. I've got toothache. Something I've bitten on board, I'm convinced. A small bone in a Chinese stirfry. At least, I hope it's a gum problem and not a hole or a stirring abscess. My dental health is dodgy at the best of times, and I'm not surprised the molar has blown up. I'm in agony, despite a couple of painkillers and an anti-inflammatory tablet. (Drugs are the first items to go into a skilled voyager's backpack. Prescription, of course.)

Paris's main airport hardly helps. Some twenty kilometres to the north-east of the city, it was avant-garde, sculpted in fashionable concrete, when it began operations in 1974. Its main terminal is a ten-storey turret that sprouts seven boarding 'satellites'. But Roissy these days is among the least practical of international gateways. A pie-shaped plan and subsequent wedges funnel passengers into tight spaces. People get sweaty and irritable. Like every aircraft criss-crossing the skies, ours is full, and we passengers, after brief liberation in corridors, are about to be concentrated yet again in an enclosed space where we will collect our baggage. And it's early in the morning. And not a lot of us have slept especially well.

Coming from Asia, we are many Chinese. Then there are the twenty or thirty Italians, all jokes and swagger, in Ferrari-red jackets and polo shirts stamped with automotive logos. I guess a works team in rally-car racing. And there are the French themselves, returning from holidays, looking great but preening — just like ducks — as soon as they are let out. Within minutes, there are too many of us waiting for luggage, the delivery of which is not Roissy's strongest suit. But we have time to spare. Idle time. Time to watch the Italians joking about the ineptitude of the French. To observe Hong Kong Chinese becoming more mystified as the minutes pass. Time in which my tooth bangs a rhythmic throb through the left side of my head. Which famous philosopher said two-thirds of the world's pain is toothache?

Backpack retrieved, I pass through customs and frontier officials in a jiffy — Roissy's biggest plus. And it seems I can push my trolley all the way to the train station if I follow what are perhaps the world's clearest signs. They're in orange, their white letters in a sharp-edged sans-serif typeface. One problem: there are simply not enough of them. The trail peters out, and I finally ask someone in a uniform. Just keep on walking, he says, right to the other end of the terminal. '*Tout au bout,*' he shouts after me. '*Au bout!*'

The walk is good exercise after the jumbo. The whole kilometre or so of it. There are stairs to negotiate and lifts to take and we should none of us ask — let alone write books about — why the cheese-eating French are so slim. How many words are needed to say 'exercise'? And manual gearshifts. And heavy shop doors that don't self-open. Even heavier office doors. Stairs in the Métro. And no snacking between meals, I'll warrant that. And no sweets, lollies, biscuits or processed fats. Or fewer of them (some younger French are changing).

The station is a transport cathedral, its floor in big grey-and-white marble tiles, its buttresses in more lofty concrete.

It smells of polished steel, and its background music is the incessant hum of escalators. My credit card fails to work at an automatic ticket machine. It's par for the course in French railway stations. I stand in a queue of perhaps twenty to reach the single clerk behind glass. There are at least a dozen more *guichets*. All unwomened. No wonder: this is the France of the thirty-five-hour week.

Back in the station itself there is little movement towards the platforms, which are a long escalator ride below. Why? In big block letters an electronic sign is broadcasting the news: since last night, it says, there has been a railway strike. English and French versions alternate. The English one is wonderful: 'Trafic,' it announces, 'is really affected'. It further advises — fairly summarily, I feel — that 'you cancel your travel'. Trains usually leave every ten minutes or so for Paris. The first one this morning will not be along for an hour. I wait, sliding about on slippery brushed-alloy benches. (But don't they look sleek?)

After my enforced wait, I'm finally in the RER, short for the regional express '*reseau*' or network. These trains are quite speedy, but how long they take to get to Paris depends entirely on how many stations they stop at on the way. And this one, being the first of the morning during a strike, is an omnibus. The dark ochre or mid-blue vinyl of its seats are hosting a forlorn *monde* within a couple of stops. Passengers are swaddled in overcoats and scarves against the unseasonal chill. Most of them have Arabic or African blood. Their glumness is contagious. It's as if the greyness of a late-autumn pre-dawn has infused their wrappings and seeped inside. They're missing the sun. It's only a few degrees above zero outside, and snow is forecast for later in the week. Very soon, the nippled floor of black rubber is obscured by shoes. Presently, you can't even glimpse the buttercup yellow of the carriage walls. And I and my backpack and my daypack and my laptop in a bag are jammed up against a window. I'm delighted younger seated passengers are between me and several standing women. I couldn't get up for them if I tried. I'm pleased that none looks pregnant. And my face hurts.

A single change to a Métro line at the Gare du Nord, a two-stop journey, and I'm out and above ground and hiking along the narrow footpath of the rue des Petites Ecuries. The day is turning out fine — 'clear and cold and lovely,' as Ernest Hemingway used to describe Parisian winter days. I'm in a fairly new building for the first half of my stay, and I bang on its full-glass frontage until a smiling Iberian greets me and lets me in. He's Monsieur Da Costa, the concierge. Like every other Parisian caretaker he is Portuguese. Without trying, and in spite of an early 747 and a late RER, I'm precisely on time to take the keys from the owner of my ground-floor studio.

'Where is Monsieur Montebello?' I ask Monsieur Da Costa. Swathed in a dark overcoat and scarf, a man of average height and thin build advances towards us from an interior courtyard. The smile on his gaunt face is wide and he extends a hand. Perfect timing, he says. I was lucky, I say, because the RER was on strike. Ah, he laughs, I wouldn't be in France if I didn't have to deal with a strike.

Now, you don't rent a studio in Paris to trip over easels, skid on spilled paint or discover naked young models in its cupboards. (If only!) A studio is simply a one-room flat, and Monsieur Montebello's is perfect for my purposes. It's large by Parisian standards, has a quite generous kitchen corner, a big hard bed, a spacious bathroom with a bath (a rarity in itself), an extendable table and a sliding glass door that opens onto a little garden in the courtyard. And it's all impeccably neat, clean and well lighted. A well-lighted room, that's what I'd been looking for. And it has been delivered. The walls are white, and Monsieur Montebello has decorated one of them with round mirrors of dinner-plate size. The floor is linoleum pretending to be strips of oak.

Monsieur Montebello says that he lives not too far away and this is an investment. He shows me the coffee machine, opening the lid to discover an old filter, filled with dregs. He's mortified, seeking my pardon several times as he disposes of it. Like many French people, he has more genuine charm than a platoon of publicists. I'd rung a few days earlier from Australia and he had been touched, he says, that I'd spoken so politely and courteously to his nine-year-old son. And Montebello? Originally from Latin precincts, his family have been French for six generations. He asks why I'm in Paris. To eat and write. And what does he do? He explains. Hmmm. Perhaps I shouldn't have asked. It sounds like a fairly abstruse form of financial advising. But, then, money and I have always been parted.

I write a cheque that amounts to a stupendous bargain for six days' accommodation in the world's most popular city. A ridiculous bargain. Is he happy with the tarif? Absolutely, he says. Now, I say, the agency dictates that I should pay you double. The bond? The *caution*? Don't worry in the slightest, he says. We can trust one another. And, on the strength of a couple of emails and two phone calls, we're doing just that. One final thing, I ask. Does he know a good dentist? Yes, absolutely, but he's a fair way away. At La Défense, the business quarter in the west of the city. I take the dentist's name and number anyway. Monsieur Montebello hopes I won't need him. 'But it'll be painless if you do,' he laughs. He must go to work.

At a leisurely pace, I arrange the apartment to my liking. I'd like to try to feel at home. For most of the next fortnight, I'll be testing Paris's legendary status as a provider of fine eating, and I hope that just being here will stimulate a few happy Gallic reminiscences as well. There is enough room to expand the table to its full width, to use one of two fold-up alloy chairs as a bedside table, to make a comfy work chair with the other by padding it with cushions from a sofa too low to use. I set up my laptop, spread myself out, and notice that one of the lights doesn't work.

I find Monsieur Da Costa in his office. Can he help me? He comes immediately. Did I try the light switch? Yes, I say, demonstrating that the switch on the cord attached to the light doesn't make it either come on or go off. No, he says, the one on the wall. He switches the light on from a wall switch two metres away. Ah, no, I say, I didn't try it. French wiring — like French plumbing — is a strange art for non-Gauls. The French do things *their* way.

Soon, my studio is perfect, a working unit, a place of no little comfort and space in a city where these things go for premium prices. For double the amount I'm paying you *might* find a reasonable, but minute, hotel room. It will have no cooking facilities, a bathroom the size of a cupboard and a shower the size of a vertical coffin. Protruding from the least appropriate spot on the least convenient wall of the shower will be plumbing that can dislocate vertebrae if you make the slightest wrong move. If you drop the soap, you will have to turn off the water and get out of the shower to retrieve it. While there is accommodation like Monsieur Montebello's to rent on a weekly — and sometimes daily — basis, why would anyone on a modest budget settle for a hotel?

The rue des Petites Ecuries is a fairly sombre and undistinguished narrow thoroughfare, a typical Parisian canyon with a ceiling — on this day at least — of chilly sky in watercolour blue. At a small supermarket nearby, I buy coffee and a packet of salt for my toothache. French supermarkets seem to deal mainly in volume, and the only salt I can find weighs in at a hefty kilo. Even if my gum was sore for the rest of my life I can't imagine I'd get through it all. Too bad.

In the nearby rue du Faubourg Saint-Denis there are food shops of all sorts, including a *poissonerie* — just what I'm after. A fat woman in a blinding white rubber apron and equally glaring gumboots is tending her seafood. The royal-blue canopy over her shop announces *AU LAGON BLEU* in big block letters — At The Blue Lagoon. There are few fillets for sale, whole fish being strewn silver and pink on deep mattresses of ice. The blue-edged display boxes, inclined a little towards the customers, put on a spectacle of esteemed bar, bream, snapper, tuna, mullets of various sorts and styles, including the prized red mullet, sole, pilchards and what appears to be orange roughy. There are also more everyday fish — salted cod and farmed salmon. Of non-fin varieties, I note crabs, squid, sea snails of a few sorts and (what I am looking for) three sorts of oysters. I want to repeat an experience I loved thirty years ago, I say to the woman. If I brought her a plate, could she open a dozen oysters for me? Certainly, she says. At your service. Probably tomorrow night, I say.

For a handful of dollars, I buy bread from a *boulangerie*, *paté de campagne* from a *charcuterie*, and a raw-milk camembert from a *fromagerie*. From a wine shop I buy a bottle of new beaujolais (a couple of weeks old) and a muscadet to go with my oysters tomorrow night.

Back at the studio, first things must come first, though, and I rinse my throbbing mouth several times in a very concentrated brine. The paté is next. In its own container of aluminium foil, it's covered with a thin lake of translucent amber jelly and weighs perhaps a third of a kilo. I chunk it onto my baguette and gum it gingerly. It's excellent — rich, meaty, very dense and tasty. But the camembert is amazingly underdone, bearing in mind its apparent softness in the shop. Its interior is still mostly chalky and it will be several days before it turns creamy. I shall be my own *affineur* of this one: I will have to take responsibility for getting this cheese into shape for eating. (This amounts to no more nor less than keeping it in a cool place and checking its maturity every day or so.) But it should come good. Everything is right about it. Its label says it's a real camembert, '*au lait cru*' and '*moulé à la louche*' — that is, made from raw (non-pasteurised) milk and ladled by hand into its moulds.

A couple of mouthwashes later, the sun has set and my gum or tooth or both are following it out of sight and mind. It looks as if the trip to *La Défense* (in defence of dental health) might be avoided. But I shouldn't speak too soon. I'm well enough, at least, to complete the day as planned. I'm on my way to Maubert Mutualité to see if I can relive my first Parisian steak-and-chips. Don't we cling to our best memories? To revisit them is a fetish; if I've had it once and it pleased me, why can't I do it a second time? Or a third? Or forever? But we can never repeat things exactly, of course, no matter how hard we try. Or that's what the, admittedly meagre, intelligent part of my mind is saying as I set off for the other side of the Seine. The rest of me is striving not to believe it.

But first, a slight detour. I come out of the Métro at Saint-Michel in the heart of the Left Bank, the busy student and restaurant quarter. I'm looking for a short street, the rue Suger, that branches off the place Saint-André-des-Arts. A Métro exit conveniently ascends into the square. And, although throngs of mainly young people — who look no different from young people anywhere else in the world in their jeans and sneakers, by the way — jostle for a cool time, the rue Suger, narrow, its footpaths mere elevated strips, is deserted. I stop at number five, where, on a rainy April night thirty-three years ago, my wife and I held our wedding reception. Then, as I recall, a wrought-iron sign above the arched doorway announced *Les Chevaliers de la Table Ronde*: the Knights of the Round Table. We descended into a medieval stone basement with massive refectory furniture. Small heraldic pennants hung in bright colours under the vaults. It all seemed authentic, and probably was. After all, around here Paris is at its oldest.

There were about forty of us at the wedding breakfast. We had booked the whole place. And I have little recollection of the meal itself, except for enormous hardwood platters of salamis and terrines and patés. Our guests seemed to enjoy themselves. There was much laughing and dancing. Tonton Camille had the best time — as he usually did at family gatherings. At around midnight, I think it was, he began a little number he used to sing, a jolly ditty. It was music-hall stuff from the 1930s and described the activities of '*ma petite Mimi*'. There were drinking games, of course, and younger revellers banged on our door — a tradition — once we had gone to bed. We missed our honeymoon flight to Corsica.

I have a wonderful memento from the restaurant: a big white page in heavy paper simulating an illuminated manuscript. I have a feeling it might have been a placemat. Across its top are jousting knights, a small audience in chain-mail armour, a castle and its keep. Under them and to the left is an exquisite 'J', decorated with Guinevere, semi-recumbent on her canopied bed and attended by three handmaidens, bidding adieu to Lancelot, who has a broadsword at his hip, a cape to his ankles and a puzzled look on his face. The 'J' is the beginning of a sentence that has fascinated me for decades: '*Jusqu'a la lie je bois dans la coupe vermeille qui fust celle du Roy*'. It translates as, 'Right to the lees, I drink from the vermilion cup that belonged to the King'. It just rings with loyalty and all that alleged honour and dignity of ancient knights' times. (In those days, it seems, the odd casual fling was exempt from scrutiny by any high moral judgements.) In wild old French below Guinevere are several lines in which she pleads her love for her '*messire*', describing her sighs and the sobs in her heart. And if, tomorrow, Lancelot fails to return from his campaigns, she says, she, a wounded bird in a cage, will die.

Number five rue Suger these days, I discover, has been recast into apartments. The ancient sandstone looks clean and dusted, as if the work has been completed only recently. There are no signs of the knights of any table — round, rectangular or oval. The heavy stone arch by which we entered is wider and more robust than I remember. And the door — massive and with bevelled panels — has been recently painted a glossy Brunswick green; a colour so deep, at any rate, that it appears almost black. Mid-door, a lion's-head holds a thick metal ring in its jaws and, inserted into the stone nearby, is a digicode panel and its buttons and speaker. So, the Knights of the Round Table have ridden off into the past. And it occurs to me that, these days, restaurants and marriages often have about the same lifespan. Say, seven years. Anywhere in the world — not just in Paris — ours is probably unusual to have outlasted the venue in which it was first celebrated.

The boulevard Saint-Germain is thronging with youth as I head east towards Maubert Mutualité. They form knots on the wide footpaths. They — and older folk — cluster in the glassed-in fronts of cafés. Many of them smoke, and the joy they have at living life in Paris froths out of the scrums like water from a cracked hose. Perhaps teased by others, one or two shriek and burst from their groups.

The boulevard widens around Maubert, which, I suspect, wasn't the case in 1971, and there is no longer any sign of the Hotel Pierwige. A recent apartment block, built in typical nineteenth-century Haussmannesque style, is where it must have been. Food shops face the street, including a superb *fromagerie* completely open to the chill night air. Opposing three-tier grandstands seat cheesey spectators in cream and grey. There are triangles and pucks and wheels. Some have surface moulds. Many of the goats'-milk varieties are coated with ashes in shades of char-grey to black. Their cities and regions of origin — sometimes even towns — are named. There are cheeses with washed rinds in colours from orange to deep mahogany. There are cheeses in shallow plastic tubs and cheeses in vine leaves tied up with rafia. Behind this stunning presentation are polished oak louvres. If you scoured Paris tonight you would find many similar shops. Cheese — its variety, nuances, flavours and complexities — is the high point of French gastronomy. Perhaps even French culture. France does nothing better.

Across the boulevard I search up and down for the bistro where I was taught to make a vinaigrette all those years ago. The Café Le Métro is not La Petite Marmite, but it seems to be the only place of similar size and status. Inside it is a stockyard of oak-panelled booths. I couldn't have been taught anything from another table in a place like this — the panels are too high. I ask for the non-smoking area. Yes, they have one, but its air is contiguous with nearby smokers' exhausts. Luckily I'm dining early and only three people — young students, they appear to be — are near. One is intent on his laptop, another scrawls longhand notes, a cigarette hanging from his bottom lip. All around are American paraphernalia — publicity panels for 'Indian' motorcycles, for instance, and a Union Pacific crest. Frank Sinatra croons. I'm served by a tall thin girl, her dark hair drawn back into a pony-tail, her eyes framed by squarish spectacles in heavy black plastic. She wears a black rollneck pullover, a tailored pale-grey jacket over it.

'You look like Nana Mouskouri,' I say. 'When she was young, of course.'

'Who is this Nana?' she says (a funny response in the circumstances, because '*nana*' is slang for a fairly libertine young lady).

'A famous singer,' I say. The waitress furrows her brow. Don't inquiet yourself (as the French verb puts it), I tell her... I'll have the *bavette* and chips. And a quarter-litre of the house Côtes du Rhone. She goes three paces before returning. The steak comes with a shallot sauce, is that OK? Fine, I say. Ten minutes later it's in front of me. It's skirt steak and is excellent — raw and red-raw inside, its taste fine. Atop it is an acceptable sludge of stewed shallots that just might have been thickened with a starch of some sort. A few ordinary lettuce leaves dressed with a weak mayonnaise and a segment of tomato are north-east of the meat. Some OK machine-cut chips are alongside them. Nobody watches me eat, I am not required to make my own salad dressing, and the past cannot be relived. At Monsieur Montebello's studio, to which I return immediately, my sleep is like death itself.

# day two

It's the old reporter in me. Start a news story with the crux of the matter. Put your best stuff near the top. I'm lunching today, at any rate, at Taillevent, the artless, the transcendent, the exemplary, perhaps the greatest, cathedral of French restauration in Paris. It's not just the food here. The experience is unique. The *hospitalité* reaches an unexpected dimension. I'm dining at the invitation of Monsieur Vrinat, its owner. The bill would break me.

I've lunched at Taillevent once before — with my wife in 1982. I'd telephoned, saying I wanted to file a last gastronomic column from Paris before returning to Australia. (I had been studying in Europe for ten months.) Dinner at Taillevent was booked out for weeks, but a lunch reservation could be made.

We arrived, and the maitre d' asked 'sir' if he would mind wearing a tie. I selected one from a range of half-a-dozen he pulled from a wardrobe in the entrance hall. It was the most extravagant of the lot, a muted rust-red *cravate* bearing miniature horse-heads like chess knights. Then we sat and ate what was put in front of us. Thin slices of sweetbreads varying in colour between pink and fawn were served with lightly sautéed wild mushrooms on the tiniest, yellow-green endive leaves. A perfect nut-oil vinaigrette dressed them. The dish cost about $A12. There were fillets of turbot luxuriating in a butter sauce containing flecks of sorrel, the herb's oxalic acid grabbing your salivaries and hanging on to balance the butter. There were scampi tails in a lobster coulis. I ate about eight big pieces of fresh foie gras of duck (about $A14) in a long-tasting brown sauce strewn with truffles, and finished with an ice flower whose petals were oval scoops of pear, raspberry, blackcurrant and passionfruit sorbets.

And the service and *entente* between the staff and the unknown Australian and his wife were exceptional from start to finish. Leading from the front was a youngish man in a sombre grey suit with, as I wrote eventually, tinted spectacles and a gentle smile. I suspected that he was the owner, Monsieur Jean-Claude Vrinat. He treated us with the greatest kindness and courtesy. And, as Taillevent emptied, I took a deep breath and asked for the bill. A waiter returned with a fold of paper on a silver salver. I opened it: '*Avec mon amical souvenir,*' it read. It was signed Jean-Claude Vrinat. The waiter had disappeared. No-one else seemed to be about. And Monsieur Vrinat himself had disappeared.

I found him on the doorstep under Taillevent's canopy in the rue Lammenais, casting an eye up and down this backstreet near the Champs Elysées. His was the signature on the bill, he admitted. I hadn't expected a free meal, I said. He smiled and said he knew it, but it had given him the greatest pleasure to offer it to us. I'd picked up a little chart of vintages in the restaurant. A footnote on it advised that it was devised by the Messieurs André and Jean-Claude Vrinat. I asked who André was, and his reply was this:

'André is my father. Like many restaurants, Taillevent has passed from father to son. People sometimes say in a mean way that a lot of sons stand on the shoulders of their fathers. Well, I am proud to say that I have stood on my father's shoulders. In our publicity material and in reference to the restaurant we always use his name as well as mine. Our regular clients like that. There is a sense of continuity about it. In everything we do we like it to appear as if my father were still here.'

These words — and the inevitability of a longer fall from your father's shoulders — ring in my ears as I take the Métro. And, for old time's sake, I go the long way — I promise myself to do it more than once during my stay. It takes me south under Paris to Montparnasse Bienvenue, where I shall change after a long walk through white-tiled vaults and bitumenised pavements, to the above-ground line to Charles de Gaulle Etoile at the top of the Champs Elysées. This line takes me past the second-floor studio where I lived for three years. I warm inside every time I pass it. But, in the meantime, there is a lot to see. Ineffably sad or janglingly boisterous is the music picked from horizontal harps in the Métro's corridors. You have to audition to play them here. So many of the musicians these days seem to be from eastern Europe. Almost all have waved goodbye to middle-age. They pluck and strike at antique instruments of honeyed wood and catgut strings. Some have CDs to sell. And almost every station is an elongated billboard, so much so that it occurs to me that Paris must be the world's billposting capital. Professional poster-hangers thrive on the Porte de Clignancourt to Porte d'Orléans line. I love watching them applying water — or perhaps glue — from buckets with broad brushes. How they unfold a hoarding at high speed from a rectangle of paper the size of a large envelope is a marvel.

At Montparnasse I must take one of the longest straight corridors of the network. Perhaps twenty metres across, three moving walkways occupy its centre. The middle one, which hurtles along at nine kilometres per hour for 185 metres, is out of commission. It was said to be a world first when it opened in 2003. Its speed was eleven kilometres per hour. Judging by the warnings, there have been teething problems. Perhaps already a brace of pensioners have been maimed in falls attributable to its haste. In Paris, you might never know. I'm left with no option but the three kilometres per hour version.

It's funny how you notice duplicates of the dead who were important to you. I used to see my father in the street or shopping for cat food in supermarkets (even though my parents hated cats). Today 'Max' Sebald, the very great German writer, who died relatively young in a car accident in 2001, is on the *tapis roulant* just ahead of me. It's Max all right, in a long grey overcoat, his spectacle frames stark, his white moustache luxuriant. His face is kindly and doleful, just like in the photographs. He's wearing a black homburg and, although none of the images of W. G. Sebald I've seen show him wearing a black homburg, I'm convinced it's the kind of hat he would wear. He observes the advertising hoardings as they pass. He would look at them this way — critically. It must be Max.

I skittle past my old studio at Dupleix — following it with my eyes — and walk from the Arc de Trimphe to Taillevent, taking a left at the rue Washington and another into the rue Lammenais itself. Nothing appears to have changed as I approach my lunch spot. The dark canopy over smoked glass doors remains emphatically discreet — on it, in roman typeface, the single word 'Taillevent'.

I'm wearing a jacket and tie today (you can't be too careful). Around my neck is an extravagant silken bolt of close diagonal checks in blue and dazzling gold that I bought at a Vietnamese street market. I am greeted by elegant young men in charcoal-grey suits, Taillevent's uniform. They are students of their boss's ineffable charisma. Monsieur Vrinat, the patron, the owner, the ringmaster of the show (two sessions daily) has had plenty of practice exercising his distinctive ways. André Vrinat opened the first Taillevent in 1946 in the somewhat-less-classy ninth arrondissement. Two years later Michelin awarded it its first star. In 1950 it moved to its present premises: a typically gorgeous Haussmann-style building in a homogenous multi-storeyed strip constructed in 1852. Initially the home of the Duc de Mornay, it was for many years the Paraguayan embassy. In 1956 Taillevent garnered its second Michelin star and in 1962, the year Jean-Claude joined the family business, its third. It has remained among France's top restaurants ever since. In Paris in 2005 Michelin ranks only nine other restaurants as highly.

Among Taillevent's most famous *habitués* have been Richard Nixon, Maria Callas and Salvador Dali. The website admits that the restaurant sometimes had trouble satisfying Dali's whims. He once asked the kitchen to duplicate an ancient recipe — unplucked peacock baked in clay. The result was disappointing and bland. The website notes that when Dali ate with his muse, Gala, they drank water. When he was accompanied by 'ravishing young women' he ordered the best wines. (Taillevent, by the way, was the nickname of Guillaume Tirel, a celebrated fourteenth-century cook to the King. He wrote *Le Viandier*, which is seen as the founding textbook of Gallic cuisine, and his coat of arms features three copper stewpots and six roses.)

Taillevent's website has prepared me for certain elegant renovations, but I am seated in a large room of gaspingly exquisite *gout* (taste). My booth is panelled to waist-height with new oak. Matching taupe-coloured leather dining chairs oppose the booths. The whole *salon* is, indeed, oak-lined with classical columns soaring to crenellated friezes. Everywhere there is richness, be it in the huge white worked napkins, the tablecloths, the crystal glassware or the silver cutlery set prongs-down, traditionally to display the flourishes of an engraved family crest. The lighting is even and faintly sepia — perfect to consume great food by.

Within five minutes, Monsieur Vrinat himself emerges from his army of servers to welcome me like an old friend. I recognise him immediately. His hair is greyer, his face a little fuller and more worn in, but it's him. If there were a world championship of charm, I'd like to be his manager, take fifteen per cent. He is so gentle, so deferential and witty, so comprehensively *charmant*, his arms lightly folded, his body subtly inclined towards his guests, his manner so quiet, earnest yet good-natured and good-humoured simultaneously. He would win by streets. His demeanour is identical, no matter the diner. Fuss is unknown here. Indeed, the restaurant's website tells you that Monsieur Vrinat wants you to feel at home in his eating place — or experience the sensation of being a hostage at the home of a dear friend (my translation). Like his staff, he wears a school-grey suit cut to the millimetre. His tie is just a little more subtle that the understated coppery check numbers of his waiters and maitres d'. His smile is genuine, beaming from a tanned handsome face, his spectacles framing lightly smoked lenses.

Monsieur Vrinat is so pleased to see me back. He has spent the summer renovating and this is the result. He hopes I like it. It is the work of the sixth architect — *sixth!* — who tried out for the job. The large windows behind me, he says, are of glass. I turn to look; they appear to be an opaque pearlescent muslin. It's glass, says Monsieur Vrinat, it really is. Special glass that admits a superlatively even and enriched luminosity. In alcoves and on tables are stark but elegant contemporary artworks — sharp sculptures of various sizes in gleaming metals. Quite a contrast to the oak.

'So, Taillevent evolves?' I say. Yes, he says, lifting a warning finger. The right word, '*evolution*'. Even the cooking.

'Never revolution?' I ask, mischievously. Monsieur Vrinat smiles. France has had its revolutions, he says. '*Non, non, non plus… Dans les revolutions on coupe les têtes!*' ('In revolutions, heads are cut off.')

On heavy cream stock of light texture, Taillevent's list is almost the size of its napkins. Think a broadsheet newspaper. Among the entrées, you may choose a velouté of grey shrimps, cauliflower and radish, a scallop salad with beetroot and citrus flavours, lobster with a cappuccino of chestnuts, and a duck *tourte au foie gras* with a rouennaise sauce. Fourteen seafood, poultry and red-meat mains follow, including john dory fillet with black olives and fennel, fried foie gras with caramelised fruits and vegetables, and a simple beef fillet with grey shallots and a top raking of salt from (no doubt) the marshes of southern Brittany. To me, the list reads modern — evolutionary — but lacking, beyond a turbot curry, the kinds of stronger and more exotic flavours we are used to in the New World.

Almost matching his boss's charm is that projected by Monsieur X, Taillevent's '*Premier Maitre d'Hotel*', as his card expresses it. With a laugh, he asks me not to identify him: 'I am called Mr No-one.' I tell him I shall eat and drink whatever he puts in front of me. I should, he says. We must enjoy Taillevent; it is a place for fun. He has been at Monsieur Vrinat's side for many, many years and to eat here is to *fête* life. People *should* enjoy themselves here, despite the restaurant's formidable reputation for refinement.

I begin with champagne and strongly flavoured gougères — puffballs made from choux pastry and cheese. A *demi-tasse* of white-bean soup with truffle oil follows, just to amuse the palate before the principal dishes arrive. It's very oily, but very tasty, too; the truffle taste not at all irksome, which it can easily be. And the first official item on the dégustation menu is a crème brulée of foie gras and small broad beans. Tanned off on top, the brulée wears a light thatch of raw apple sticks about a millimetre square. An oval of crisped bread of about the same thickness accompanies. The blend of liver and beans is very subtle indeed and quite sweet. Soon, I am regaled with a great chablis to accompany three ravioli in a shallow bowl of tawny foam. The foam is a 'cappuccino' of chestnuts, and the ravioli — made with fresh, soft, thin, translucent paste — contain pieces of wild cep and girolle mushrooms infiltrated with chestnut crumbs. Each of these fungi has a characteristic flavour, and at Taillevent they sing their parts distinctly against the chestnut's sweet creaminess. Taillevent's culinary style is obvious. It's slightly sweet, but the flavours are huge. Big flavours are fine as long as they are in balance. And they are here — any palate funambulist could tell you. The cooking assembles tastes that are firm yet subtle, and I'm now looking forward more than ever to chatting to its relatively new and young chef, Alain Solivérès.

Do the people eating around me know how good Taillevent is? The place is packed, and many have more than an inkling, I decide. The lunchers' average age is over sixty, and you can assume that many have known Monsieur Vrinat for years. Exceptions are the American couple — a handsome young executive and his elegant black companion. Each would hold a significant position, I guess, in a financial institution of some sort. Or a UN bureauracy. Then there are the suited businessmen in their mid-forties in the next booth. Lean and elegant in that wholly Parisian self-regard, they face one another across a shared table, exchanging financial intelligence, talking about oil prices and movements in trade indices. 'Do you speak Spanish?' one asks the other. There is work down there, apparently. And it might seem curious to us that these two men, who seem to rely on and know each other well and who obviously interact a great deal professionally, use the formal '*vous*' form of 'you'. It's a mark of respect, we must understand, a declaration of trustworthiness while their career meters are running. If they were dining as host and guest in one another's homes, these same two men might use the familiar form, '*tu*'. There is simply a lot more to lose — a lot more at stake — during work hours than when relaxing. Relationships must be more clinical and considered so that it is easier to impose conditions. And harder for others to betray them. Most of us betray only those closest to us.

Every now and then, Monsier Vrinat checks that I'm fine. He tours his dining room constantly, always a kind word ready — even a longish conversation with a well-known guest. My next dish is a big fillet of lightly fried, exquisite red mullet resting on a *brandade* (a fine mince) of 'merlu', which is a cousin of whiting. A paper-thin wafer tops the fish, and the lot is presented on the most delicate, luminous green and minerally herbal juice that, in turn, is retained by a rectangle of very strong garlic mayonnaise. The amplitude of flavours again surprises. They are astonishingly strong, yet perfectly balanced. With a wonderful disc of stuffed lamb saddle I eat potatoes of a density and sweetness that defies culinary logic and miniature halves of artichokes whose aniseed savour is reluctant to leave the rear palate. And, in a tall-stemmed martini glass, I finish with a layered delight of vanilla cream, rose-faint jelly containing bits of ripe fig and a cloud of snow egg. A crowning deep-fried figleaf hints at veiling the concoction's muted immodesty. All the while, my table is periodically swept of crumbs with a sickle-shaped brush of worked silver and its matching pan.

You might be curious about Taillevent's prices. What does one pay to eat in this princely way in such regal surrounds? Two decades ago, the cost seemed reasonable. Today, the cheapest dish on the list is the grey-shrimp velouté — it costs 34 euros, or about $A56. The scallop salad costs $A7 more. The red mullet dish is 62 euros (about $A103), and the turbot curry with Malaga raisins and coconut milk, among the more expensive offerings, comes in at 90 euros (about $A150). For two people, the list's most expensive dish is roast Bresse chicken with truffles and a walnut butter — it costs 150 euros. Desserts are priced at 24 euros.

Monsieur No-one drops by with a story. He rides a scooter to and from work. When he got off it near his apartment the other night, a beggar approached him. There was something about the man that made Monsieur No-one immediately sympathetic to his plight. He found four euros in his pocket and gave them to the man, suggesting he go and get a good hot coffee. And the tramp replied, '*Merci, mon bon monsieur.*' ('Thank you, my good man.') It was not good French, something a French person would never say, of course, says Monsieur No-one. But he was very touched by it. '*Merci, mon bon monsieur,*' repeats Monsieur No-one, grinning, as he drifts to another table. '*Merci, mon bon monsieur.*'

I have eaten and drunk sublimely, and it remains only to quiz the man behind it. Alain Solivérès approaches me across the dining room, a recognisably working chef from his stained white tunic — name embossed — clogs and matted thatch of blond hair. He looks a little tired and glows with half-evaporated sweat. Of medium build, he speaks in a soft, modest and confidential manner. He is forty-two and has been chef at Taillevent for almost two years. A perfect age, I think, to reach such a pinnacle. The new list is his seventh, and I was right to detect the restaurant's culinary evolution. Taillevent's regular clients were ready to accept it, he says. But he had to respect the place. '*Lieu*' is the word he uses, signifying a reverence for one of the holies of gastronomic holies. He has been so bold as to take the lobster *boudin* (sausage) off the menu. It had been a signature dish for thirty years. I quiz him about the light sweetness of even some of his savoury dishes. It is purely accidental, he smiles. No sugar is added to savoury plates. Because we are in autumn, root crops possess higher and more concentrated sweetness. It has to be that.

Monsieur Vrinat gives him carte blanche to write menus. But the boss no doubt takes an interest in them, I say. Certainly, says Alain Solivérès. But he trusts him. After all, he has, since beginning his apprenticeship in 1979, already had a long career that includes stints with other culinary magicians, among them the Alains, Ducasse and Senderens. In almost a decade before joining Taillevent, he has won a second Michelin star for Les Elysées du Vernet at the Hotel Vernet on the other side of the Champs Elysées.

And what about Senderens, I ask, who a year or so back declared in print that French cooking was losing ground to more inventive concoctions in the New World. Are French chefs too timid and rooted in tradition? Alain Solivérès draws breath and pauses for quite a while. You must cook as you feel and as you were trained, he says. If you were brought up to eat McDonald's you would cook like that. He has Maltese and Algerian ancestors; cooking and eating are part of his culture. And Taillevent, the '*lieu*', has to be respected. There is a 'war' between French and fusion cooking styles, yet each needs to express itself. And what of the froth and foam chefs, the chemical concocters? It is 'laboratory' cooking, he says. Monsieur Solivérès seems to have little interest in it.

I say that I liked his strong flavours. There were some mammoth tastes, especially with the vegetables. Yes, he acknowledges, but it is all in the raw materials. Taillevent takes delivery of vegetables three times a day. He thanks me for coming — for appreciating what he does — gets up and returns to the kitchen.

I finish with strong fine coffee and miniature cakes and chocolates. Then, with charm so skilled it seems effortless, Monsieur Vrinat shows me out. I remind him of the twenty-three years between visits and he laughs. 'Don't leave it that long again,' he admonishes, and I promise I won't.

With a bit of rummaging, I manage to find a large platter among Monsieur Montebello's crockery. At around 6 pm I revisit the Blue Lagoon. The big woman isn't there, but two equally hefty blokes in early middle-age are serving customers. They too are enveloped in huge white aprons, their feet gumbooted brighter than white. Pale-blue fleeces squeeze out of the aprons and up around their necks like cats through a crack in a wall.

Holding out the platter to the server I judge to be the more senior of the two, I explain again what I want. He knows exactly. A dozen oysters? No problems. I look again at his three sorts: *belons*; *fines de claires;* and, a little more expensive, the generic '*huitres de Normandie*'. They nestle among seaweed in trapezoid boxes stapled together from raw plywood slats. Make it eighteen, I say, getting greedy despite my lunch. Six of each. I reason that the Taillevent meal will be well and truly digested in an hour or so, but I should show it some sort of gastronomic respect by declining food of any complexity for dinner. Just stick to something simple, light and unspeakably refined. The oysters are a perfect choice, a gustatory pinnacle, but also devoid of the palate differentials that might spoil my immediate memories of Taillevent's tucker. I am anticipating at this very instant their juiciness — indeed the flavour of each variety. *Belons* are flat indigenous bivalves that have a big characteristic taste — lots of iodine. They're not to everyone's *gout* but I love them. The *fines* and the more expensive 'Normandy' oysters will taste similar, be equally succulent but slightly different in size.

I ask to take a few photographs, and the men joke about their looks. Doesn't everyone about to be photographed? '*C'est pour L'Equipe?*' shouts the boss, posing as a front-row rugby gorilla in the hope of appearing in Paris's famous sports daily. I'll be back in an hour, I say. He assures me that my oysters will be ready.

Ninety minutes later I pay just over 13 euros (about $A20) for them. They've been carefully opened, their lids replaced over juices brimming in the bottom half-shells. A few strands of seaweed steady them strategically. I take special care to keep the plate horizontal in my two-hundred-metre walk back to the studio.

I uncork the muscadet (*sur lie* — I'm no expert, but it sounds as if lees have had something to do with the wine-making) from Sèvre et Maine. It's a sharp but fruity little drop whose colour, says the label, is a '*belle robe limpide aux reflets verts typiques*' — 'a clear beautiful colour with typical green hints'. Its aroma is supposed to be frank and fresh with citrus touches, and in the mouth it's fruity, ample and rich. After a *bouchée* or two, I find myself agreeing with the whole pitch. And the muscadet partners the oysters brilliantly. The shellfish are unsurprisingly exquisite. (And I chew — and swallow.) Without a doubt, they have come up from the Normandy coast very early this morning. The Blue Lagoon probably bought them at any time between 1 and 6 am, when the immense fish market at Rungis on the outskirts of Paris is in full swell. Each oyster is firmly and naturally attached to its bottom shell. You must cut the gristly little 'foot' to eat it. Squeeze lemon juice over oysters if you like — I have no lemons tonight — but I prefer them as prehistoric man discovered them. I notice one further indication of their freshness: live barnacles encrust most of the top shells. I count eighteen on one shell alone. Their vulval shape arouses me even more than the oysters. But a greater tease are the tiny feelers that protrude from the barnacles, wave about, then quickly retract when I tickle them. Barnacle clitorises?

I insert a CD of Brahms's first piano concerto into my laptop. Oysters, muscadet and Brahms? Elitist? Pretentious? Believe it if you like, but I'd disagree. And I'm alone, what's more, trying to impress nobody. I'd just say that life is short. Quality in all things is my chief concern. I once drank a bottle of calvados while watching, on a scratchy black-and-white television, Glenn Gould play Bach's Goldberg variations. I count it among my greatest life-moments. It was his last shot at them, as it happened, a recital for Canadian TV. He died soon after. So it's oysters and Brahms rather than a Big Mac and Kylie. Depth rather than the shallow end. A big hit rather than a little one. Complexity rather than simplicity. At bottom, value in return for my time and money. I'm mean, you see.

But the CD has links to Paris, too. The pianist is Julius Katchen, the wonderful American artist who died of cancer here in the spring of 1969. He was forty-two. In my youth I collected pianists. Well, not their bodies and souls, of course, but their 'live' — as they say these days — performances. (It occurs to me, by the way, that so many 'live' rock performances are actually stone dead.) On one occasion, I collected Julius. He strode on to the platform of the Melbourne Town Hall in a white tuxedo with a scarlet buttonhole. Carnation, if I remember rightly. He was a great smiler at the audience, but when he got down to business his artistry was transcendental. And he played Brahms's first piano concerto as only he could. It was magical; a perfect interpretation of the composer's sad majesty. As it is on this recording. I once saw a documentary of Katchen's life — how the New Jersey boy of northern European origins eventually adopted Paris as his home and was taught here by the legendary Nadia Boulanger. (Nadia the baker; now there was a piano teacher!) The film showed Julius and his wife walking in the Champs de Mars, near where I used to live, and my heart was warm and heavy. In the background he played the exquisite second Intermezzo from Brahms's opus 118 piano pieces. Nobody has ever played it better.

So, it's a night of sweet sorrow, wonderful oysters, Brahms's limping dignity and too many glasses of muscadet. I begin writing notes on my laptop, pondering why so many great pianists have died young — Glenn Gould, Geza Anda and Dinu Lipatti, to name a few that instantly come to mind. And Julius. A short intense life is better than a long vacuous one, I decide, and pianists — all solo musicians, in fact — must concentrate enormously if they are to succeed. They can't afford to relax. Perhaps that has something to do with it? Perhaps they put more into a few years than most of us put into a lifetime? Perhaps they just wear out? Perhaps people who live so intensely also anticipate their deaths more keenly? I reread my notes. Perhaps I've had too much to drink? I've gone on about people who can play Beethoven's Diabelli variations; they have premonitions. Of pianists who appreciate Bach and the late Beethoven sonatas having a kind of death-knowledge and therefore a death-wish.

But what's all this 'kitchen' stuff with a lower-case 'k'? My computer is thinking for me. How dare it! It's trying to *help* me, for God's sake! *Me*, who spells to live. It's changing my 'Katchens' to 'kitchens'. How *fucking* dare it! I feel like smashing it on Monsieur Montebello's lino. A laptop with intelligence! Give me a break! Ridiculous! Respelling my words! How dare it! What does it know about Julius Katchen? Fuck all!

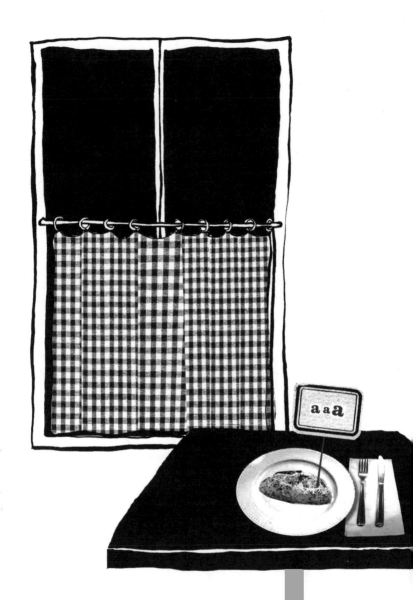

# day three

Sorry to disabuse you of a popular notion, but most French almost never eat croissants for breakfast. The Gauls I know eat fresh air, washing it down with strong black coffee. They rarely have time for anything else, time being the commodity in shortest supply in Paris. The popular image of the French sitting down to wicker baskets lined with red-checked gingham from which spill freshly baked croissants is somewhat misleading, then. They eat wonderful Parisian pastries at weekends, when they have more time. So I can't really tell you who eats all those croissants — not to mention the other bakery items — in the windows of Paris's hundreds of *patisseries*. Perhaps tourists or newcomers to France. I like breakfast, and I like croissants and especially *pains au chocolat* or *pains aux raisins* (sweet pastries filled with a slim inner cylinder of chocolate or plugged with raisins).

Monsieur Da Costa is in his poky office in the corridor. I ask if he knows any good pastry shops nearby. The one up on the corner is said to be good, he says. 'Who says?' I ask. Madame Da Costa, he says with a broad grin. Mind you, he adds, he's never tried anything from there... He doesn't eat breakfast.

I take a left and walk perhaps eighty metres. A tiny corner commerce, La Daube *patisserie* should be more about stews and wet dishes (being what *daubes*, the cooking pots and that which is ladled from them, are all about). But it's a tiny pastry outlet all right, with floor-to-ceiling glass shone to a starshine, its floor tiled in glazed terracotta. A limited range of pastries sit on steel racks in glass display cases.

I choose a croissant and a *pain aux raisins*. The latter are sometimes called *escargots*, because they swirl like a snail's shell. Studding the helix and its stiff pastry-cream are the dried grapes, which look — if you let your imagine run away a little — a bit like dead blowflies. The croissant costs 70 cents (euro cents, of course) and the escargot 90 cents. I put down a five-euro bill.

Serving me is a smiling young Frenchman of north African descent. He is as neat and tidy as any of the French nationals of umpteen generations (and many ethnic backgrounds) that you will find serving in the shops of Paris this morning. Ironically, his frizzy hair is as closely cropped as a Jewish — or Catholic, if you like — skullcap. He is polite to a fault. And he looks at my note, leaving it on the counter, and rummages in his till. I offer to try to find change, digging into my wallet. Don't worry, he says, and, after several seconds, he renders 40 cents. The five-euro note remains on the glass top. And I say, '*Sur cinq?*' ('From five?') Of course, he laughs, apologises, and corrects his mistake immediately, finding three more euros for me and putting the fiver in his till.

Now you can perceive this little scene a couple of ways. First, that it was an honest mistake — as I'm convinced without a shadow of a doubt it was. But there are many long-term ethnic French who would gladly take it differently. The Arab — notice the word 'Arab', not 'north African Frenchman' — tried to cheat me, they would say.

I am visiting France at an interesting time. In recent weeks, hundreds of cars have been set alight by young men, mainly of north African origin. Just a fortnight ago, night-rioting occurred in about 270 communes across the country, probably the peak of the disturbances. Thousands of police tried to maintain order, arresting hundreds, and a reported 1400 vehicles were torched. The streets of Paris, in particular, are still not calm. Where I'm living — north of the river and heading towards the notorious northern suburbs — the north African population is substantial.

All of this is in reaction to a another reckless reaction. Minister of the Interior, Nicolas Sarkozy, a presidential candidate in 2007, is the main culprit, although prime minister Dominique de Villepin and other government members and officials are not without blame. Two teenage boys, Bouna Traoré and Ziad Benna, were electrocuted in Clichy-sur-Bois, north of Paris, while allegedly fleeing from police at the end of October. They had scaled the fence of a sub-station. Several of France's most senior politicians said it was their own fault. They suggested that the boys or their friends were implicated in petty thievery that might have been occurring just before they were killed. But many commentators, including several representing the French Left and, most powerfully in English, *The Economist* and Jeremy Harding in the *London Review of Books*, have argued that the rioting would not have spread so widely if Monsieur Sarkozy had refrained a few days earlier from describing troublemakers in another difficult Parisian suburb as '*racailles*'. Look it up, and you will discover, as Larousse puts it, that a *racaille* is a 'vile person'. If we were seeking an English word, he would be a hoon, a lout, a hooligan, a rabble-rouser or a troublemaker. Naturally, French north-African youth took offence at this. They hurt for no fault of their own.

At the heart of the matter are the housing estates in which they live — high-rise ghettoes in outer suburbs flung up after the war to accommodate immigrant workers and, in 1962, *pied-noirs* (French born in Algeria). In an ideal world, immigration should correspond with work opportunities, but few French governments have tackled well the problem of blacks and north Africans obtaining the right to live in France on the grounds of family reunion. Mr Harding cited a 2003 statistic: 6000 people were given residency in France to work, but 80,000 went to join family members already there. In short, they need jobs as well as families. And respect, I might add.

At the time of writing, 750 suburbs throughout France are classified as 'sensitive urban areas', and about one in three of the young people who live in them is unemployed. National unemployment in France is a little under ten per cent. But perhaps the most disturbing thing about the riots is Monsieur Sarkozy's popularity: he mollified his tone, but his hardword approach to the north African problem has been immensely popular with many European French.

I pick up my change. The croissant and the *pain aux raisins* are delicious. Both are very buttery, the pastry of the croissant so flaky and brittle that to eat it is almost like crushing unsalty salt flakes. It's all right for the Inuits and their twenty words — or however many they have — for snow. I wish there were more for pastry. I rethink: the croissant's crusty exterior is somewhere between sandy and flaky. Eating it is like eating a form of crunchy melting-butter sand. Pointless, isn't it, to try to describe some things? An important distinction in types of croissants is made in pastry shops. There are plain croissants and croissants *au beurre* — with butter, if you like, or, more accurately, made with extra butter. I've been criticised in Australia for spreading butter on croissants (then following it up with my homemade plum jam) and I can see why. The pastry of the *pain aux raisins* is similar; the pastry cream stiff and sweet and the fruit swollen and juicy, not overcooked and dried out as it can sometimes be.

Here, at the beginning of my adventure, I'm taking no chances. Get a few early runs on the gastronomic scoreboard. You won't believe it, but eating in Paris is often just plain boring, and can even be dodgy. So Chartier is my lunch choice. I have eaten here many times and trust it with the French classics. More than likely, I shall have to queue to get in. You often do. Tourists and Parisians alike form an orderly cord outside its wide revolving door. Inside, more will be waiting for a free table.

Chartier is an easy, relatively short walk from my studio (Monsieur Montebello's studio — and I write that with a tinge of envy). I take the rue Richer, the continuation of the rue des Petites Ecuries, then turn left into the rue du Faubourg Montmartre. Chartier is fifty metres up a cobbled lane near the corner of the (grand) boulevard Montmartre. Its entrance is nondescript, basically an archaic revolving door with a many-paned window alongside boasting numerous accolades from value-for-money restaurant judges. Inside, two attractions dominate: its simple good food, which is amazingly cheap, and its ambience, which takes you back to the nineteenth century. Cheap? Chartier arguably offers the best value-for-money eating-out in all of Paris. I know of no better place. And once you're seated at one of Chartier's ranks of tables covered with butcher's paper, you'll feel very keenly that you are experiencing something authentically Parisian.

In the nineteenth century, Parisian butchers with business acumen would brew up a hearty broth from offcuts and sell it to customers. Some of them expanded this sideline, offering simple dishes as well as their soups. Eventually, some gave away retailing meat altogether and concentrated on providing cheap, traditional menus in large dining rooms. These places came to be known as *bouillons* or 'boil-ups', a synonym for the broth that started it all. French middle-classes are the world's champions at spotting and following trends, and *bouillons* soon became so popular that they eschewed all modesty and transmogrified into full-fledged restaurants in grand venues. Never were their origins forgotten, though, and simple orthodox French dishes continued to be served. And at cheap prices. Camille and Edouard Chartier had a chain of *bouillons* on both sides of the Seine in the 1890s. The Faubourg Montmartre flagship is the last.

The place is packed. Every place at every table in this gorgeous high-ceilinged space seems taken. I'm led to a table for four — a couple are just leaving — and seated alongside a husband and wife from Bordeaux. (You learn these things quickly at Chartier because, even if your fellow diners don't introduce themselves, everyone eavesdrops on everyone else's conversations.) Out with the notebook.

Under the butcher's paper are pink-and-white tablecloths in a tea-towel fabric. The chairs are well-worn basic timber bistro jobs and the stainless steel cutlery and glassware are rudimentary (indeed, my knife is more bent than a Kings Cross cop). Paper napkins are standard, and the floor is in brown linoleum. Tables butt-join, and you share big baskets of baguettes cut up into generous slices, salt and pepper, oil, vinegar and mustard with anyone within arm's reach. Above me is an ancient hat-and-pack rack of three brass tubes.

But look beyond your table for the real joy of Chartier. Bevelled mirrors pattern the walls in a dazzling check. The massive columns supporting the high ceiling have been stained chocolate so many times now, it seems, that they appear encrusted. Chartier is an eating-out relic. A small earthquake might set it to tumbling down, but Paris is in little danger of that, geographically speaking.

Small boxes on the walls were once for *serviettes*. They are numbered, and used to be coveted by Chartier's regulars. At some time in the past, authorities quite rightly ruled them unhygienic and these days they are empty. The ceiling has a magnificent skylight surrounded by a border of ornate wrought iron, and the light here seems remarkably even, if slightly jaundiced.

I'm settled in for less than five minutes before one of Chartier's black-bowtied, black-waistcoated waiters of a certain age — as many of them are — seats a woman opposite me. She is, I'd guess, in her early thirties, has long dark hair and wears a heavy anorak. She carries a daypack with a koala attached to the zipper. She's looking all around in awe and wonder, a nice smile of achievement at having discovered Chartier written all over her face. I smile back across the table. I notice pink pompoms protruding above the heels of her sneakers. Her lower calf is ringed with a tattoo of names in a fine cursive script. The chest of her coarse-knit pullover undulates with a promotion: 'Fun-knee gril', whatever that might mean.

'Australian?' I ask, because one of your obligations at Chartier is to talk to the others at your table.

'Nooooo!' she insists with an immense smile.

'I noticed the koala,' I say, pointing at the backpack.

'I got it in Cairns,' she says with the Midwest twang of a cheerfollower, if not leader. At least *I'm* Australian, I laugh. She's Sioux, she says, offering her hand across the mustard pot and vinegar and oil bottles in their perforated sheet-metal holder. From Boise, Idaho. This is her first time in Paris, and she has read about the famous Chartier and how cheap — and good — it is and she's finally here. She beams. Sue, I repeat, and she says, yes, but it's spelled with an 'ioux' because she's mostly Indian. Red. I strain to detect racial indicators. There is something of stolid serenity in her visage, a gently noble nose and longish brown face.

'You'll like Chartier,' I say. Yes, she certainly will, she enthuses, but she's really not used to French food and wants to order something she'll find easy. She wants only an entrée. You mean a main-course size? Yes, she says, that's our entrée. It's a starter, I say, in France and lots of other countries. It's the *entry* to the meal. With justification, she looks at me sideways, then scans skywards to take in Chartier's filigreed iron.

We peruse the list. It's of almost A3 size and chronicles a plethora of offerings under the rubrics '*poissons*', '*plats*', '*legumes*', '*fromages*', '*desserts*' and '*glaces*'. And that's not counting starters (on any given day Chartier has twenty of them). Turn over to find a limited, but cheap, list of French wines — a bottle of Chartier's own *'rouge de table'* costs 4.90 euros. Things like a boiled egg with house-made mayonnaise costs 2 euros, as do salads of tomato, cucumber and red cabbage. You'll pay the same for grated carrot with a lemon vinaigrette, and a slice of what is known as Parisian ham — just excellent basic ham for us — with sour gherkins. Terrine and jellied pork dishes cost a little more, and I always have the dark maroon, dense and salty Bayonne ham.

But none of that helps Sioux. She likes fish, she laughs, because Boise is a long way from the sea. It's her lucky day, I suggest, because *'raie'* (skate) with a caper sauce is on special for a mere 9.90 euros.

'Ray?' she says. 'Is that like a fish with wings?'

'Exactly,' I say. 'In fact, they call it "wing of ray".'

'Like in stingray?' she asks.

'It's wonderful,' I say. 'Not at all what you think.' She looks somewhat anxious.

'Yes, but you know, I've snorkeled, and a stingray just surprised me out of nowhere once, and, oh my God, I nearly died when I saw it… So big and all glidey… It just kind of flew past. It was sooo close. I nearly drowned…' Sioux begins flapping her arms up and down, which amuses the couple from Bordeaux, who are listening to our conversation with the most abject and bemused expressions on their faces.

I explain that skate is not exactly stingray — probably a third cousin and much smaller. Sioux draws on her brave Indian progenitors and orders it. I take the Bayonne ham followed by another of my favourites here, the *andouillette* sausage.

Three slices of ham with a knob of fresh half-salted butter and plenty of bread are wonderful. I dive into the breadbasket repeatedly and, when it's half-empty, a waiter replaces it with freshly cut slices. Sioux goes off amid the crowds at other tables and snaps away with her digital camera. She is especially taken by the smell and the look of the old and, like me, has noticed the gee-gaws of tumbling plaster oak leaves high up on the walls and the magnificently ornate 'C' for Chartier, which accompanies them. There's nothing like this in Boise, she says, rather stating the obvious.

Sioux is an actress (sometimes), a very good (on her own admission) cocktail mixologist at other times, and quite a handy waiter. But for the moment she just works and saves to travel. It's her way of getting an education. It will improve her acting. Couldn't agree more, I say, and I also couldn't help noticing the names on her calf, even in this cold weather.

'They are my most important people in the world,' she says, 'and I like to know they're near.' She pokes out her leg from beneath the table and hoists the hem of her jeans. A finger traces around the names. 'Charleen is my mom,' she says, 'and Doris is my grandmom. Then there's Aunt Gladys.' She smiles and lets her cuff drop. Close by in time of need, I say. A mom is a girl's best friend. Sioux smiles.

The skate looks excellent. Pretty plating is no great preoccupation at Chartier, yet here is a thick piece of wing with capers, chopped chives and small tomato cubes in what appears to be a vinaigrette sauce. Three boiled potatoes attend the fish, and they will have excellent flavour — all French potatoes do. And there is a clutch of the world's greatest green salad, *mâche*. My *andouillette* — grilled chitterling sausage — is accompanied by a formidable pile of chips.

'You know?' says Sioux, 'I took the '*raie*' because of the capers. I know capers. We sometimes put them in martinis. You know martinis?' Yes, I say, and I love them made with vodka straight from the freezer.

Sioux tends to her wing delicately, coaxing its soft fibrous texture onto her fork.

'Ray always looks like the cross-section of some kind of advanced aircraft wing, doesn't it?' I say. She looks at me strangely. Her face lights up. It's good, she opines, teasing up another forkful. I try it. Its flavour is full, and the sauce nicely rounded and lightly oily. Sioux is looking at my *andouillette* suspiciously. I've yet to split it open. She wants to know what kind of sausage it is. I suggest that perhaps she wouldn't want to know at all. 'Try me,' she declares. Well, it's a sausage made mainly from the lower bowels of pigs.

'Oh, *gross!*' she says.

'Now,' I say, 'I'm going to split it, and you'll see, if you look, a great many curls of bits of guts and other stuff tumble out onto the plate. And you might smell something a little… "agricultural?" But don't be alarmed. And you don't have to watch. It's kind of adult-rated food.'

I take my knife to the *andouillette*. Curls of gluey skin-pale guts spill out, and the characteristic, gorgeous whiff of a shitty pigpen rises all by itself from the plate. Sioux is mesmerised. Thunderstruck. Appalled. She pulls a face. She sniffs the air. Tentatively.

'Oh my God!' she says. 'I can smell it… Oh my God! I can! You can't eat that!'

I smile and shrug and eat, and the *andouillette's* innards are sensationally gluey and flavoursome and gelatinous. Sioux is devastated. I can tell by the despairing look on her face. She sees me as odd, perhaps more beast than human. Mostly primitive, at any rate. She has stopped eating her skate. She glances at the *andouillette* and looks away. She no longer wants to sit opposite me. Her 'experience' at Chartier has been spoilt forever. And I'm the culprit. I feel awful. She looks around the room. Two tables away there is a vacant space next to three young Frenchwomen who are gabbling and gesticulating, densely involved in office politics, no doubt.

'I'm really sorry,' says Sioux, picking up her plate of fish and her knife and fork. 'Really sorry. I just can't… Just can't… That smell is so gross… It's the smell mainly… I'm sorry.' And she moves in alongside the Frenchwomen.

Just my luck, but Chartier is like that. On a good day you can eat well and learn a little about quantum physics or selling

Citroëns in Reims, listen to a diatribe about French taxes or hear Britons boast about the strength of the pound (they think nobody understands them). But Chartier is always fun, a living treasure. In 1996 it celebrated its hundredth birthday. And they do something here that was common thirty years ago: the waiters tot up your *addition* in ballpoint on the butcher's paper covering your table. I suspect they take lessons in the ornamental scribble they rip onto the paper. And the speed at which they compute mentally would dazzle today's teenagers. I keep my bill as a memento before heading home in this especially damp and cold early winter.

Word-of-mouth is the flywheel of most successful restaurants. I guess it's the same with books and films and any creative endeavour. We believe what our friends and those we trust tell us. And one person in particular who knows his food has mentioned Fogón to me. It's Spanish, its cook is Spanish and you begin with some tapas dishes, then have a rice — paella-style — main course. Simple. But the cooking is very original and super-refined, I'm told. I'm a little dubious.

Over the years, I've had two extremely bad trips eating paella. In a Melbourne restaurant many years ago, a seafood paella smelt strongly of ammonia. Many of its marine bits were off — well and truly on the rot. I was reviewing the restaurant, ate little of its paella and the place failed. Then, holidaying on the Languedoc coast in the early 1970s, I went with a brother-in-law to Barcelona to see a bullfight. Opting for the complete tourist experience, we ordered paella for lunch. We sat and sweated in a dingy café under a creaking fan that clacked with every rotation. A recorded loop of flamenco music repeated itself until I felt like shooting the guitarist. I think now — though I might be wrong — that men with Zapata moustaches lazed about drinking sangria. The waiters certainly lazed about. They had, as well, surly Iberian manners, even if their moustaches were more disciplined. And Pierre and I waited. And waited. And waited. Eventually — I think it took more than an hour from ordering to eating — a shallow iron dish about half a metre across was put in front of us. In it, bits of protein of indeterminate species and yellow rice drifted in tepid oil several centimetres deep. The result was something truly revolting, disgusting, and we left most of it for the café's cat. (Who, I'm sure, left most of it for the café's rats.)

A good critic tries not to prejudge, it goes without saying. And I believe I'm successfully repressing any paella memories as I take a seat at Fogón. (It's on the Left Bank not far from the Saint-Michel station.) I want to be up on the Champs Elysées by around 9 pm, I tell the waitress. I've been invited to the Lido. Fogón looks as if it knows its job. It's a narrow walk-in place facing the Seine and, like most restaurants cramped for space, it has chosen to illude optically by surfacing one long wall with mirrors above benches richly upholstered in a coppery satin. On the white-painted facing wall are more mirrors — horizontal in bronze-painted frames. It's contemporary: even, rectangular tables in oak, white fabric mats covering them. Facing the benches are luxurious white leather dining chairs.

Two slices of an excellent crisp-crusted brown sourdough arrive in a grey hessian sack the size of a toiletries bag. And when I can't find my cutlery, the waitress tells me knives and forks are in the drawer. *Effectivement*, I say to myself, finding a clever little compartment concealed in the table top. They contain stainless steel utensils I am less happy with — they have squared-off ends that will dig into my palms, especially the left, if I hold them correctly. I see bad cutlery everywhere these days; someone has let *designers* loose on knives and forks. They shouldn't have. There's a good chance, I reflect, that the creative people are Scandinavians or Italians. I mean, all that Beowulf blood still flows in the Scandos' veins; their ancients ate with their fists and broadswords. And, as we all know, Latins eat spaghetti with their fingers.

Fogón's list is brief; to the point. It's on the right-hand page facing a slim inventory of wines on the left. You can begin with *charcuterie* — pork products — that are made from Iberian pigs raised in the mountains, it says. Why not the seaside, you might ask. Humans enjoy the seaside more than mountains, in general, so wouldn't pigs be the same? Wouldn't the odd piggy-dip — a bit of porcine surfing — do them the world of good? I understand waves break on the north-west Spanish coast. Well, the mountains, as Europeans would presume when reading Fogón's list, means hardy aromatic plants on which an Iberian alpine pig might graze. This notion is central to the marketing of Corsican *charcuterie*, for instance. Undermining this is a menu note saying that Fogón's pigs eat mainly acorns. I can see them now, lazing under a giant, hospitable tree. And one says to the other, 'Wow, these acorns, Luís, my son! Just sensational! Throw me another.'

You can order a serving of ham for 25 euros, chorizo sausage or salami for 10 euros and ham *rillettes* (fat and shredded pork) for 12 euros. Below these offerings are six types of rice cooked paella-style: with squid, squid ink and calamari or with vegetables for 18 euros, or with ham for 23 euros. But the rice dishes, the list notes, are for a minimum of two diners. I explain what I'm doing and mention the people who have recommended Fogón. No problems (it's an international expression, I'm afraid), avers the waitress. We'll do a rice for two and you can eat what you like. Now, she asks, *charcuterie* or tapas? The list offers a 35-euro menu — several tapas dishes to start, followed by a rice and a finisher of choice. Again, it's for a minimum of two, but I argue my case and opt for it. No problems, she says.

In a short while, I'm eating, beginning with a deft crystalline consommé of ham, chicken and mint, a subtle, tasty soup. Four small cubes of swordfish are next. They've been marinated in vinegar for half-an-hour, I learn, then coated with a very thin and fine dust of flour and deep-fried. They're wonderful. A croquette of Iberian ham demonstrates the complex flavours of this superlative product, but it's pretty dull alongside the swordfish. And it's a little too salty at that. Two big mussels are barely cooked and excellent, and a baby calamari is wonderful. These tapas, I must add, are not alone on the plate. Each dish has its sophisticated garnishes — grilled red capsicum slugs, thin slivers of root vegetable and garlic. Three cylinders of huge octopus tentacle on a timber skewer are miraculously tender and tasty — the best legs I've eaten. Strewn with salt flakes, they share a rectangular dish with a block of shreddy, crunchy eel-and-potato pie and a groyne of spicy green-tomato chutney. A scallop in its shell is excellent, springy and tasty, but it's topped with squiggles of ham (no doubt, Iberian) and salt flakes, which makes the dish far too salty, in my view. Moreover, a tawny froth in the half-shell that has fungal hints is also too salty. Tentative conclusion: salt is important to Iberian cuisine? (Over many years, I've found European cooking generally far saltier than what I'm used to in Australia.) Three large and shining chunks of persimmon speckled with herbs are the pick of the tapas. They're draped with a balsamic reduction and have been marinated in lemon juice and oil, I learn. They're great — soft, fruity and sharp, a true expression of the art of balancing sour, salt, sweet and bitter. Vanilla, says the waitress, is in the reduction. And lime. And 'secrets'.

So far, mostly good. Fogón is showing off some stylish culinary conjuring indeed, but the oversalting is a pity. I'm left to digest my tapas for an appropriate fifteen minutes before a shallow iron dish thirty or so centimetres across arrives. It's supported above the table on a three-legged stand made from steel of little-finger thickness. From first glance it lacks appeal. Very hot, it's liberating an unappetising and volatile, salty, cephalopodic odour. The smell verges on astringency. It's a little sickening. And the food itself appears to be somewhat dry. The rubbly surface of the rice and the little rings of calamari are coated with a skin like cellophane.

Into it I dive, deciding immediately that it's too salty for me — way, way too salty. The calamari's delicate taste has been all but obliterated. Tomatoes and carrots seem to be contributors to the dish, but their flavours are lost. The rice is *al dente* (firm on the bite) and saffron's presence is over the top. Like truffles and balsamic vinegar, saffron is one of cooking's bullies; you have to keep it in order and, in my view, Fogón's kitchen hasn't. I don't like the paella's colour: it's an intense mid-brown, which suggests overdone-ness in food like this. Out of politeness, though, I eat perhaps a third of the dish, not enjoying it. I shouldn't do it, I tell myself, but I do. And after a morsel of cheese and quince paste, I'm out of Fogón for 47 euros, including a fino sherry and a glass of fairly basic white wine. Were my informants right about Fogón? Well, yes — and no, I reflect. Close, but no cigar. And paella, it appears, still stalks me.

In the Métro to the Lido — nice song title that — I begin belching. Every minute or so I erupt, ejecting gas. I pick up my complimentary ticket at the box office and take my place at a back-row table. I concede that I'm not in the best shape to enjoy this famous *spectacle*, as the French call it. But I accept the offer of a flute of champagne. I wrote to this famous veteran of Paris's *fol* side a few months ago, telling them what I was doing. And why. When I went to live in France in the early 1970s, one of my first Gallic experiences was this place. I have very fond memories of it. I went with my fiancée. To this day, the colour, costumes, choreography and coordination of chorus-line crumpet constitute a lasting souvenir. And the shameless bare breasts! They were unbelievable. An Australian Methodist boy was up to his neck in a new and thrilling tease-zone. It was a world I could not possibly have imagined — as foreign to me as the topography of Venus or an extra-terrestrial civilisation.

Being French, my fiancée saw it all as fun. Me? It disturbed me. How others live when you're brought up to think

everyone is a committed, conservative and repressed Christian
is beyond knowing and understanding. I was an Inca seeing
Pizzaro and his men. In no way, said Dominique, could the Lido
be misconstrued as provocative. Or even naughty. Under her
guidance, I changed my views very quickly. Such are cultures.
The evening's single fault was an ordinary dinner — I
remember a particularly gristly and quite thin bit of steak. This
time the Lido has offered me a seat at their new show *Bonheur*,
hoping I will enjoy it as much as my first experience.

Paris and naughtiness are a traditional pairing, of course;
part of Gallic lore. I own a slim volume called *Paris by Night*.
The book is cloth-bound in rich violet (the colour of the silk
that lines a cad's cape, say), the title impressed on the cover
in gold leaf, three stars twinkling around it. Published in
1959, it depicts — mostly through black-and-white
photographs of nude showgirls — Paris's nightclubs and
cabarets. Unblushingly outrageous, the book describes itself
as a 'tour of the capital's gay pleasure haunts' (my research
suggests that 'gay' began to mean what it does today some
time in the late 1960s). *Paris by Night* appears to have been
written by a Frenchman, Jacques Robert, but was translated
by Stephanie and Richard Sutton, who might or might not
have been anglophones. Whatever the case, the text gushes in
a style that predates by several years the time when young
women came to be considered human beings and not simply
sex objects. Exhibit one: 'The Night-Prowler is a patient
hunter anywhere, but in Paris he will wander until the grey
light of dawn tinges the sky, waiting and searching for that
frivolous heavenly moment which he will be able to recall
thirty years later.' Exhibit two: 'On nights such as these the
prowler suffers from an almost unquenchable thirst. He
becomes a lion, a man-eater, and it is well known that lions,
even as man-eaters in fairy-tales, are always avid for the
freshest flesh, young, and preferably well-padded.' Even the
captions indicate a long outdated perspective: Marguerite is

'charming and most promising'; Monique Gérard —
photographed astride a balustrade — 'tore her first underwear
on the rails of the Sacré-Coeur steps'; a shot from a dance-
floor of legs and pantied pudenda explains that 'Bluebells
look charming from any viewpoint'; Sidonie Patin, a
performer at the Crazy Horse 'is just eighteen'; and Linda
Romeo, unlike many girls, 'can also pilot a plane'.

The Lido is described as 'the supreme queen of her
Species, a Venetian Palace in the Catacombs of Elysium'.
Founded in 1929 by Léon Volterra (who had originally intended
to open a Turkish bath), by 1945 the Lido was the finest cabaret
in the world. Pierre-Louis Guérin, one of Volterra's partners,
told the author of his 'perpetual wish to astound Paris...' One
night he would present a 'Carnival of Venice, built on a so-called
Lidorama with Panoramic scenery'. On another, he might 'pour
artificial rain on a battalion of nude women'. He staged ice
shows in the middle of summer, and his extravaganzas were
routinely backed by three or more orchestras. Then there are the
Lido's iconic Bluebell Girls, the 'most famous girl-troupe in the
world...' In 1959 the most intriguing of them was Antoinette,
'who wears glasses'. At management level, it seems, 'the problem
of whether Antoinette should appear nude with or without (her
glasses) was hotly disputed'. Jacques Robert himself advised the
Lido that she should wear them. 'Such a thing had never been
seen before,' he writes, 'and it turned out to be incredibly sexy.'

Well, years pass and, if I'm looking for excuses for being
picky, it might be because I didn't have indigestion thirty
years ago. Still, several hundred of us are sardined into a gently
sloping auditorium. Despite freezing rain outside, it's close and
smoky in the *salle*, which is dominated by red and black plush
that is worn in places. A bit tatty. The tiers of tables are gently
arced, and at ranks below me diners finish their meals. The
whole place is quite dark, of course, with illumination provided

mostly by quaint skyscraper-like table lamps — obelisks in red and white perspex shards. A six-piece warm-up band is on stage fronted by a *chanteuse* in a long, black dress split high to the thigh. The boys on the trumpet, sax, guitar and drums are in tuxedos and bowties. They look bored. She's singing famous French torch numbers such as *New York, New York*.

I begin counting how many *spectateurs* are smoking, but drop the ball, numerically speaking, at sixty-three. The rest of us passively inhale. One of the great lessons the New World is teaching the Old is implementation of smoking bans. France remains somewhat backward in this matter. But it's better than some of its neighbours. The spectators finishing dinner have paid between 140 and 200 euros a person for the meal and show, including champagne. For 80 or 100 euros (depending on the day of the week) you can watch the show and drink a half-bottle of bubbly. A dance floor in front of the band hosts two or three shuffling couples, and in style and substance I suppose you can get the same thing a great deal cheaper at, say, the Dubbo RSL.

I sip my champagne, hoping it might ease my frequent belches and a tightening abdomen. I'm not feeling at all well. But I console myself; the tooth trauma has passed, and this one will too. With luck, sooner rather than later. I'm about to see the Lido's twenty-sixth spectacle, its brochure tells me. It's the story of a woman seeking happiness. (Sound familiar?) It will take you 'on a ninety-minute journey of emotion and discovery with images that will fill your eyes and your imagination'. Four tableaux feature the Bluebell Girls and the Lido Boy Dancers.

In fact, the show is pretty boring and my indigestion gets worse. The costumes are extravagant and colourful, but from another era. They're silly. The staging is conventional. Basically, young and gorgeous bodies march straight lines or circles and occasionally rotate or high-kick. They wear funny hats, ridiculous head-pieces and apparel you wouldn't chance even at a Melbourne Cup. There are girls in top hats, girls in Thai-style fretworked headgear and girls in pink feathers. Girls in enough feathers, indeed, to fly. One scene clearly represents a street, because the girls and boys are in streetwear. With one exception: a strategic area of the girls' suits has been blown away to reveal their breasts. If their grins weren't so broad, it occurs to me, they would resemble stupefied survivors of a nuclear attack. Lots of coloured lasers pierce the blackness above the audience. The star of the show, who has a good body but never gets her gear off — I suspect she is slightly more senior than the Bluebells — has a smile of cast-iron. Sometimes she sings flat, and it's impossible, anyway, to tell if she's *chant*ing or miming. She is backed by voluptuous music, but I can't see an orchestra. Moreover, unlike Richie Benaud's suntan, there's no story here. No narrative. Just pointless scene after pointless scene. And if they went head-to-head on precision, the Lido Boys would beat the Bluebell Girls. Indeed, the girls are so sloppy on occasion that they'd be easybeats for the North Montana Linedancing Association's B-grade team. But I'm not denying their bodies.

Wonderful independent acts punctuating the 'narrative' save *Bonheur*. There's a couple who do some miraculous figure-skating at enormous speed on a square rink the size of perhaps half-a-dozen dining tables. A tiny woman contortionist runs through The Book of Knots on a trapeze, and a bloke tangles and untangles himself from a bolt of white satin hanging from the flies. Now, all these are great — and worthy of the name 'spectacle'.

Perhaps it's my indigestion, but I leave disappointed. I would hate to have paid. I leave my second glass of champagne untouched and my back hurts, I realise. The Lido's dining chairs sit at right angles to the stage, and you must twist your body accordingly to get front and square, as they say in football.

I belch all the way back to the studio and hit my drug kit as soon as the key is out of the lock. An anti-inflammatory for my back, a very rare second Omeprazole tablet (it reduces stomach acidity) for the day, and half a Valium for sleep's sake. Looming, though, is the thought that I'm iller than I think I am.

# day four

I'm alive, but only just. If I'm awake at 5 am, I must be alive, I reason. Last night's sleep was restive, and I've done little of it. I'm blurry from the Valium, my stomach is cramping constantly, and I'm still belching. My rear end is making quite a fist of all four Mozart horn concertos. I'm a wreck. There's the awful chance, I realise, that I'm too ill to do anything gastronomically constructive today. But I should try. I struggle out of bed and manage to swallow a dried crust from a two-day-old baguette. I'm lightheaded and want only to go back to bed. I know I should try to find extra antacid tablets in the nearby supermarket. They'll be a backstop (I'm wary of the consequences — unsure about them — of overdosing on Omeprazole). I barely manage to down half a glass of water before struggling into a very cold rue des Petites Ecuries.

I should have guessed. The supermarket has no indigestion tablets. Everything in France has its place. Everything is attributed according to good commonsense, basic Cartesian rationality. And indigestion tablets, I guess, would be sold only by pharmacists. It would be *their* territory. You buy pork products from a *charcutier*, not a *boucher*. I haven't got the energy to go down to the rue du Faubourg Saint-Denis to find out. Could my tumultuous intestines be reacting to Paris's tap water? It would be unusual after three days drinking it. And I drink it without problem whenever I'm here. But I buy a big bottle of mineral water, just in case, and return to the studio.

Everything I do is at the discretion of my cramps, it seems. Liquefy me, and the gas would fuel the traffic of France. I sit. I stand. I review the work I should be doing. (Have I mentioned my Methodist upbringing?) I try to read. I look at the bed longingly and think, quite fairly, that lying down means throwing in the towel, running up the white flag. I'm ill, but I'll blast through. The only blasting I'm doing, of course, I've already mentioned. At 12.30 pm I give in and take to the bed.

I'm prostrate for no more than fifteen seconds before a need — an undeniable desire — overwhelms me. I am thankful for it already as I sprint five metres, kneel on Monsieur Montebello's fake-oak linoleum and grip the rim of the lavatory bowl with two hands. Then paint it. Violently. You've seen Jackson Pollock work? Fast and arbitrary. There's a man who could sling paint. My raging at the porcelain is similar. Talk about Barry McKenzie's Technicolour yawns. Pieces of carrot emerge still in the small cubes into which Fogón's kitchen had chopped them. Tomato — and perhaps red capsicum — are intact smears. Hundreds of rice grains — thousands, it seems, but that's wrong — show no signs of fraying. Even the tan of last night's paella has been retained. I vomit repeatedly for perhaps a minute. And muse that the result is pretty. It could be a new *faience* pattern from a Gien dinner set. But I find it hard to cope with the intact rice grains. I am astonished. Disbelieving. I calculate that I've been trying to break them down for sixteen hours. Has Fogón's rice been digestion-proofed? Sprayed? Of course not. But the paella didn't like me. Pays me back for not liking it, I suppose.

I am exhausted; completely debilitated. But much better with the source of my discomfort evacuated. And I go to bed, deep sleep taking me at one o'clock in the afternoon as, beyond my window, Paris itself is changing gear from busy to frantic.

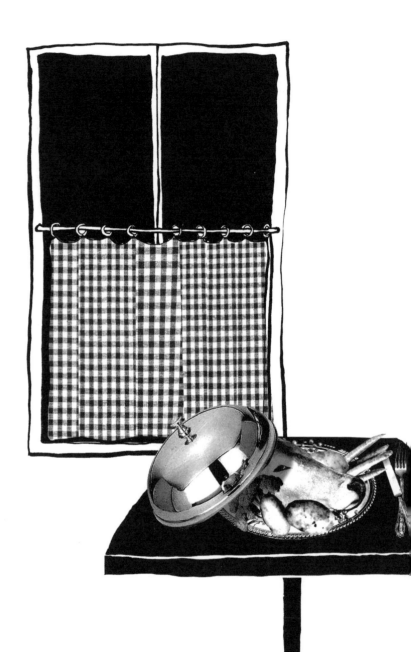

# day five

I wake early, feeling as fragile as a rickshaw-wallah's singlet. But the cramps have gone. And the belching. My delicacy will depart, and by lunchtime I shall be fine, I know. I had better be. I'm anticipating an enormous pleasure today: a *dégustation* by arguably Paris's biggest new culinary star. Pascal Barbot won a first Michelin *macaron* (the round almond-paste biscuit by which French chefs call Michelin's honours) for his restaurant, Astrance, the year it opened — just five years ago. His second is only months old. Moreover, he cooked for two years in Sydney and is the first French chef to revere Australia's culinary contribution (essentially the appropriate assembling of diverse ingredients) to world gastronomy. Without prompting, he told me on the telephone a few weeks ago that his years in Australia had definitely influenced what he was serving diners at home.

So I'd better be well. My stomach is empty and will stay that way until I take up implements at Astrance. Previous tenants of Monsieur Montebello's studio have left a couple of commercial soup sachets containing the dried makings for a broth. I use one. An Italian brand, its foil packet depicts lots of flourishing colourful vegetables. Of good, strong and complex flavour, it's also salty but not too much. I eat an end of bread. By now it's as hard as a dinner plate and I gum it into a paste I can swallow. (My tooth has completely recovered.)

It occurs to me that when events like last night happen, it's a bonus in my job to have delicate guts. The inflammation and ulceration (discovered only four months ago and subsequently healed) of my oesophagus is, in all probability, mostly genetic: my father died relatively young of gullet cancer, nine months after his first gastroscopy. But another trump is the alarm bells that ring in my stomach whenever food is wrong. Whenever it starts upsetting me. That's probably a skill I've developed from extremely varied eating.

I take the same route for Astrance as for Taillevent. This time, though, I shall get off the Métro at Passy — posh Passy — the first station after the train crosses the river via the pont de Bir-Hakeim. I'm noticing many more police in the Métro's passages this trip, no doubt because of the riots. They're in twos and threes and wear combat boots and a kind of dark denim coverall, pistols and badges bright. They stop young north Africans and blacks for their papers. Males only are quizzed. Their female companions complain from a safe distance. I overhear a baby-faced *flic* (cop) ask one Arab youth how long he's been in France. 'Six years,' he replies.

Max Sebald is missing from Montparnasse's *tapis roulant* today and the nine kilometres per hour lane is still out of order. Soon I'm on the viaduct, passing my old studio, which I can't help staring at until it is out of sight. (It's always shut up these days. Moreover, a fake plastic stained-glass effect that covered the kitchen window and that I rather liked has been removed.) Then on to the bridge, and Passy, which is an elevated Right Bank precinct several metres above river level. Going towards the Champs Elysées from Passy, you disappear straight into a tunnel and re-emerge only on foot. This is the sixteenth arrondissement, built on a hill. Here the streets are wider, the immigrants fewer, and the seven- and eight-storey apartment buildings have an elegance and authority lacking in more modest parts of the city. Their stormwater downpipes are made of heavy fluted iron, wall brackets ending in ornate collars. The fawn-and-grey stone exteriors are grooved between courses, and corbels that support balconies are often ornately carved. Around Passy, building maintenance is impeccable and constant.

I walk up the hill to the place de Costa Rica, and turn right down the wide and elegant boulevard Delessert. Few people stroll the footpaths this bright cold day. Halfway along is a broad stone staircase descending to the rue Beethoven, in which I shall find Astrance. It's a short street, and I can't see any obvious restaurant signs along it. But I'm early, and I've got time to do the block, continuing along the boulevard to the Trocadéro garden and the avenue du Président Kennedy by the river. I photograph the Eiffel Tower soaring up between trees in full leaf.

Two-Michelin-starred eating places aren't generally as tiny as Astrance. I'm surprised at this small, square but very elegant space. I'm the first in for lunch, and a grey-suited, long-tied waiter takes me to a corner table. He is in his late twenties, I'd guess, and his neat haircut appears recent. I'm there for no more than half a minute before two more young men join him to look over paperwork — a sheet of reservations, I'd guess — at the small bar inside the door. They appear to be in their early thirties, but might be older (French young men and women always look younger than their ages). The taller of the two is elegantly grey-suited. The shorter, who has close-cropped black hair, wears a white chef's tunic, an aubergine apron over it.

I get up and ask if I can take photographs before the lunch crowd arrives. The men oblige without hesitation. And it suddenly dawns on me as I snap away at the striated grey walls, the benches and seats in cadmium-yellow leather, the rich fabric tablecloths and napkins and a minuscule mezzanine behind a nautical balustrade… No, it couldn't be.

He's surely too young to be Pascal Barbot, Astrance's chef and owner? I glance at him and he smiles. His face has the rosy-cheeked gleam of a first-year university student.

'Monsieur Downes,' he says. 'Pascal Barbot,' and I stride over to shake his hand. He acquaints me immediately with his business partner, the older of the two young men in suits. He's Christophe Rohat, maître d'. We exchange briefly the usual jolly nonsense, then I tell him I can't believe the size of Astrance. It's twenty-five seats, he says, and it's what they want. Quality is more important than other considerations. They'd rather do twenty-five *couverts* well than hundreds badly. We talk about Sydney cooks and restaurants we know and about where he worked in Australia. And does he think, I suggest, that his time in Australia has influenced what he cooks here? 'Perhaps you'll tell me after you've eaten,' he says, confidence counterpointing deference. We laugh, he returns to his kitchen, and I'm left in young Monsieur Rohat's hands.

A presentation plate of hand-blown glass containing swirls in a rosewater colour is in front of me. North-west of the plate is a squat glass vase containing a yellow rose and two orchids, one of them a deep purple. Beneath my feet are large ceramic tiles with an ancient Greek-grey appearance. Mirrors on the walls are simply framed in brilliant gold. A silvered alcove has glass shelves supporting stamped and numbered black bottles of cognac, their wax seals broken. They date from the sixties and seventies.

Then the dishes begin to arrive, all matched with wines selected by Monsieur Rohat. On a plain glass square, a spoon contains a perfect mound of what I'm told is parmesan 'cream' topped with a couple of tiny thyme leaves. To its left is a thick oval of toasted *brioche* (a light cakey bread) drenched with rosemary butter. Simple and unspectacular, these palate amusements are sharp scrub-ups, especially the parmesan. Next up is what appears to be a small glass of a very frothy beer plated on a white saucer. The head is a clementine (a sort of mandarin) mousse, the beer a carrot-flavoured yoghurt. The concoction is very cold, the flavours terrifically strong but foiling one another perfectly. I love it. It's witty as well, unpretentious, laughing at itself, and therefore unlike a lot of top Gallic cuisine.

Let me leave for a while Astrance's ultimate confection — an artless and brilliant piece of culinary work that came next — to summarise the rest of the meal. I hope I haven't miscounted, but I *dégusted* six savoury dishes after the signature. Two huge scallop adductor muscles — as sweet and springy as you could get — present on a small mound of spinach in a curry-flavoured froth. In a second small bowl, raw worms of scallop swim in a brilliant fungal consommé. (A few flakes of pink Murray River salt from Mildura on each scallop would make a formidable dish sublime, I think to myself.) Two oysters as plump as cushions wade in a mussel sabayon. They wear slivers of ginger and red capsicum and crumbs of roasted nuts. It's very Australian, but the mussel sabayon would probably have been stronger down south. And the ginger's contribution a little more robust. There's a fillet of *sandre*, an esteemed cousin of perch from the Loire River. I wish the world who loves eating could see its colours. In the middle of the cross-section, the flesh is mauve, then, like a rainbow, the hues change to indigo, a blue-pink, then pale pink and finally a creamy white near the skin. And the meat shines, glinting irridescently like a slick of oil. Its taste is mild, but it's real and wild and accompanied by very thin slices of raw and fried *cèpes* (a gill-free mushroom), a cylinder of fried apple, a small ovoid of a herb purée and another of nuts and garlic.

Alongside me, a jovial couple of amateur eaters in late middle-age appear to live locally. I admire them, because they're the French who are prepared to try these very different and adventurous tastes. This is antipodean style, I'm tempted to tell them. Luckily for them, I shut up. He's dressed splendidly, a shirt of possibly two-fold Egyptian cotton — has to be — in yellow and mauve stripes taut across his considerable *embonpoint*. He wears braces, a silk tie in a rich saffron and a dark suit. His spectacle frames are in striped perspex. Perhaps he designs *sous-vêtements* for well-heeled women. His wife looks impeccable, as do all French women of a certain age. When they're out, that is. It takes work. And he says to her that this food is the product of someone performing a *métier*, what we might call a profession that you put your heart and soul into. He talks about its creativity. Then he says something I am especially pleased to hear. He observes that the dishes are put together with a certain '*génie d'association*'. 'You've got it!' I almost scream at him. 'You can see what young Monsieur Barbot is on about.'

Australian chefs are showing the world that ingredients don't need to be blended into anonymity for cooking to have occurred. Prepared appropriately, they can associate with others on a plate to produce a pleasing integrity. And that's what you are getting at Astrance. I eat *lotte*, another freshwater fish, with translucent discs of pumpkin, turnip and white radish, a clementine emulsion, and a partnering bowl of *oursin* (sea urchin) coulis and raw urchin leaves. Paper-thin slices of a huge white truffle arrive over meat juice, and duck breast comes with bright fried vegie bits, black olive crumbs and leek choppings, eggplant topped with a sweet miso paste and duck liver spread on toast. There's a chilli and lemongrass sorbet — the flavours more restrained than they would be in Australia — and the star of the desserts is a plonk of quince jelly blanketed with a sabayon of bitter almonds. Monsieur Barbot's cooking shows comprehensive technique — at this level you expect nothing less, of course. His mousses, froths and jellies are super-refined, sauces less emphasised than they are in more traditional French *haute cuisine*. But it's his *assemblies* of flavours and textures that make him braver and more interesting than most chefs working in Paris today.

And what of the signature dish? It reminds me of a wedge of Australian meringue layer cake, except that this one is composed of two levels of pale-fawn foie gras marinated in *verjus* (halfway between grape juice and vinegar) and three of very thin white slices of big field mushrooms. A 'dust' of dried mushrooms covers the top, looking a bit like cocoa powder. The confection is originally a puck constructed to bread-and-butter-plate size — four servings per puck. It sits on a base of millimetre-thin crunchy biscuit in a slick of walnut oil. A lightly bittersweet lemon purée makes a groin to the north-east. It's so ridiculously simple but such a huge treat. I grieve as I finish it, which happens rarely.

Pascal Barbot joins me after service. I congratulate him on his dishes, recognise their Australian characteristics, and rave about his foie gras 'cake'. Yes, he says, it's perfect for a signature dish because foie gras and mushrooms are available all year around. Unassuming, Monsieur Barbot says he is just doing his job and loving it. He's happy with progress. Because the place is small, his team can concentrate on quality. (He's thirty-three, Christophe Rohat a year older.) There's a two-month waiting list for dinner and a three-week one for lunch.

I suggest the Murray River salt on the scallops. He is delighted. He'd love to have such a product and wants me to email him a contact. He was five years at Alain Passard's three-Michelin-starred restaurant, Arpège. Passard, who crossed over to vegetables in 2001, eliminating red meat from his carte, is his greatest influence. But he also worked with Alain Senderens. He was two years in London and a year in Noumea. We talk about his years in Sydney. He was responsible for cooking the dinner list at Tony Bilson's Ampersand overlooking Cockle Bay. Sydney liberated his culinary thoughts. It freed him in the head — '*dans ma tête*'.

The Australian style is a natural phemonen, he reckons, in which cooks don't question whether oysters, ginger, leeks and peanuts go together, they just do it. Assembling diverse foodstuffs is part of Australia's gastronomic heritage these days, a phenomenon he believes is about twenty years old. (He clearly bothered to find out such things when he lived in Australia.) In Paris his cooking has to be a little more restrained than it might be over there, he says. You *can* introduce exotic ingredients in France, but this country has a convention of butter and cream, and you have to think of your clients. He likes to play what he calls 'little notes' of unusual foodstuffs in his culinary music. He passes on a short list of the Parisian restaurants he likes, and I promise to send him an address for Murray River salt.

And the cost of what I ate? Once again, I've been a guest, but for a meal at Astrance you will pay, says Michelin, somewhere between 70 and 150 euros. Reasonable, under the circumstances. Strolling back to Passy station, I'm surprised at how light I feel — even after such a lunch — and how enthusiastic I am at discovering new taste delights. How much I'm enjoying the ride! Just as well. I have reserved a test-run of one of France's greatest dishes tonight — *tête de veau* (veal's head) — at a small restaurant renowned for its rigour in upholding the great tradition.

The mother of the same Pierre with whom I shared the dodgy paella once asked me — when I was new to France — if I ate absolutely *everything*. It's a common enough question here. Yes, of course, I said. At the weekend, she said, she was doing *tête de veau*, a great favourite with the family. My new wife and I had been invited to their country cottage, quite a substantial house, as it turned out, on the tailored banks of the Loing canal at Montigny, south of the capital.

Madame Veschambre was a champion cook, and a weekend at Montigny consisted mainly of eating and drinking. The *tête de veau*, as I recall, was a lunch event. (It had to have been, of course, lunch being traditionally more important in France than dinner, especially for families.) The sun shone, light flooded the dining room, the french doors were flung wide and the silver-grey canal flowed nowhere in particular in the middle ground, beyond flourishes of blue hydrangea. Time gets in the way of recollection and I can't now remember what we had for starters. (We most definitely would have had starters, probably salamis, terrines and other produce of the fermented pig.) And I can't recall, even, if the *tête de veau* was served French-style, piled high on a huge communal plate in the middle of the table. (It almost certainly was.) Madame Veschambre insisted I get the best bit, though, a nice slice of cheek. Within seconds it was in front of me. And I looked and couldn't believe what I saw. A closed eye socket, the upper lid heavily lashed, was mid-plate. I smiled politely. I toyed with the dish for a few minutes, eating around the socket, before giving up. Madame Veschambre sliced some fresh ham to replace my *tête*.

I'm recalling this shameful incident — the shame on me — during the five hundred metres I need to walk on a very cold night to find Le Pré Cadet in the rue Saulnier. (But in those days, I tell myself, I wasn't a professional eater.) Le Pré scores a single spoon and fork in Michelin. But it's one of only forty eating places in the city's twenty arrondissements rated a 'Bib Gourmand'. In these, you may eat a quality meal for 33 euros or less, without drinks. Its *tête de veau*, says Michelin, is the pride of the *maison*. It's certainly a modest place. Its name is in plain block letters on windows hung with curtains of white gauze, a model sailing ship in one of them.

Inside, it's of handkerchief size. Already, most of the closely packed tables host spirited *convives*. A middle-aged man, plainer in appearance than a bureaucrat's briefcase, darts around the room like a hummingbird after nectar. Indeed, I can't recall his face or the way he was dressed as I write this only weeks later, but I hope Michel Le Boulch won't mind my saying he was probably in a maroon sleeveless jumper. Or grey. I'm sure he had a plain long-sleeved shirt on. None of which is relevant to the *tête de veau*, of course.

He sits me down in the centre of the room near a square column with mirrored surfaces. I run through again what I'd mentioned on the phone when I made my reservation. He's fascinated: an Australian who wants to write about *tête de veau*. He darts off and returns with a cutting from a Parisian newspaper lauding his restaurant and its wonderful traditional dishes. He will fax it to me. His sole waiter joins us to gawk at the Australian who wants to write about *tête de veau*! (Let me add, by way of context, that many French might ask you, even these days, to which countries Australian doctors go to get their training. Or if we really do eat only gum leaves and boiled mutton.) So I am from outer space. But within minutes they are aware that I know a little, and I am shown the utmost deference and respect.

By the sounds of the conversations around me, the diners — perhaps the place holds about twenty-four — are equally English and locals. Perhaps Le Pré has been written about by a London newspaper. A table of six Frenchpersons in front of me, however, has an empty chair. In bubbly mood, their word-plays are becoming cleverer by the empty glass. They're waiting for a birthday boy, I overhear. He's had to drive back from Meaux, his wife tells the others. Oh, says a chap with a ruddy complexion shone like one of the Sun King's walnut tables at Versailles, he takes his hat off to him in this frigid weather and at this hour. Dashing back for his birthday dinner. Hmmm, he adds. Perhaps he'll win a *prix de Meaux*. They all roar with laughter: *brie de Meaux* (the cheese) and *prix de Meaux* (there's probably no such thing) sounding similar.

Le Pré Cadet's little bar inside the door is so cluttered with bottles, notices, posters and paraphernalia that it's almost obscured. The dishes emerging from the kitchen seem to come from that direction, too. The rest of the restaurant is just plain cosy. The chairs are solid, a deep red and upholstered, and red-brown felt covers the floor. Tables are double-draped, first in a heavy cardinal cloth, then a yellow one. The big fabric napkins match the top cloth. The ceiling and walls are painted yellow, and naïve-style art in pencils and pastels that I don't think is very good hang on them. On a very modestly priced list, not a single dish deviates from the Gallic straight and narrow: twelve burgundy-style (garlic and butter) snails cost 16 euros; herring fillets with warm potatoes (9 euros); a whole avocado, half filled with crab meat, the other half with yabby tails (10 euros); roasted sole (24 euros); sweetbreads (25 euros); fillet steak with a green pepper (not capsicum) sauce (25 euros); and a '*véritable andouillette*' with Meaux mustard costs 19 euros. I order the *tête de veau en serviette, et les sauces* for 24 euros.

'You've labelled the *andouillette* 5A,' I say to Monsieur Le Boulch. 'I've seen the same sort of thing in other restaurants. What does it mean?'

He begins a tortuous alliterative journey. It stands for an association that certifies the quality of the sausage, he says. It's the… He tries once. Twice. Draws breath, tries again to get the name right. His young waiter intervenes. Monsieur Le Boulch left out '*amicale*', he offers. They decide finally that the five capital 'A's stand for the *Association Amicale des Amateurs d'Authentique Andouillette*. Or perhaps it's '*andouillette authentique*', says Monsieur Le Boulch. And Duval, his supplier, is one of the best. I'll have to return another night, I say, as they dash off to serve other customers. I'm left to wonder how many snags worldwide have their own shotgun-riding associations.

Accompanied by big slices of crusty brown bread, a pot of *rillettes* (pork shreds and fat) is Le Pré's *amuse-bouche*. Some *amuse-bouche*! The fires are well and truly stoked, appetites sated to a degree, by the time you get to entrées.

Monsieur Le Boulch and I discuss wines. The just-released beaujolais *nouveau* is not very good, he says. Nonetheless, he pours me tastes of this and two other beaujolais. He hopes a Morgon 2004 won't displease me. He's proved correct.

The birthday boy arrives and there is much kissing and back-slapping. Arnaud says you must have won a *prix de Meaux* to get here roughly on time, says his wife. They laugh even louder at the joke's rerun.

Under a huge silver cloche, my veal's head arrives. Monsieur Le Boulch scintillates with pride. He lifts the lid. There is enough food on a yellow napkin under the cloche to feed New Zealand. Sprinkled with fresh parsley choppings of erratic sizes are enormous logs of steamed carrot of intense colour, boulders of steamed spuds and enormous, pale and translucent treads of meat from a veal's head. You see, he says, it's the real thing. Everything's there. With a serving fork he begins poking, calling the roll as he goes. Brains, cheek, tongue and '*oreille*'. I mishear. What? '*Oreille, oreille,*' he insists. He tugs at his left ear. Oh, yes, I laugh. Of course. Onto the plate in front of me he forks enough food to last me a fortnight. It seems not to have reduced what's on the platter.

The young waiter arrives with the sauces — classics called *gribiche* and *ravigote*. They're homely, rough-chopped concoctions in stainless-steel kidney dishes. A *gribiche* contains hard-boiled eggs, oil and vinegar, mustard, sour gherkins and soft green herbs, mostly parsley. The *ravigote* is a shallot-infused white sauce very rarely seen these days. It's flavoured with herbs — mainly chives, but also tarragon — at the last moment. I look for eyelashes. There are none. Bearing in mind what I've eaten already today, I do well to try a little bit of everything. Soft, sweet, gelatinous, perfect in every classical way, but, yes, I'll grant you, eating this kind of food takes stick if you're not used to it. And I'm always worried about indigestion.

The lights dim and Monsieur Le Boulch marches to the birthday-boy's table holding high a cake stuck with five spitting and hissing sparklers. We all sing Happy Birthday, and the birthday boy, all smiles, bows to the room. I stall on the veal's head. The sauces are so good, though; so deeply rooted in family and what it stands for — ideas of incalculable value for the French.

Monsieur Le Boulch has had the Cadet for sixteen years, he tells me. Before that he owned the Bar des Artistes, which he sold when his wife got ill. His chef, William Dhenim, has been with him forever. I tell him how much I enjoyed the head. He's only doing his job, he says. Now, he suggests, I should finish off with their just-made apple sorbet, calvados (apple distillate) poured on top. How can I resist? Monsieur Le Boulch pours the liqueur with embarrassing enthusiasm over three orbs the size of tennis balls. They're excellent, with a fruitiness so fresh it squabbles with my tongue, and cost me the grand sum of 6.50 euros.

Many French restaurants of modest persuasions battle hard to do well, partly because French home cooking is often excellent. The Pré Cadet, for instance, serves what you would get from the most talented of home cooks. Nothing more nor less. Add Monsieur Le Boulch's authentic hospitality, and you're almost at the hearth on a freezing night. And without the washing-up to do afterwards.

# day six

I need a swim. A swim followed by a long walk. I have gone without any semblance of real exercise for days. I'm going to promenade nostalgically today, revisiting one or two favourite haunts. But before I start, a swim. The nearest public pool is not too far, in the rue de Rochechouart. I've got a bathing cap that I never use in Australia, knowing they're obligatory in France.

Low and diffuse leaden clouds seem to hover in the icy air just above the tenth's mansard roofs. They're menacing. Threatening. I'm at the pool in ten minutes. It's part of a municipal sports complex, one of several around Paris, that appears to have been built perhaps in the 1970s judging by its concrete brutalist style. You pay 2.60 euros and descend several flights of stairs to the water. I find the idea of a public swimming pool well below street level — buried in a dungeon, if you like — unnerving. A bit spooky, as Dame Edna might say. It reminds me of Herbert Read's green child leading Olivero by the hand into the grotto and the caves of the dead at the end of the story. 'The water had no sooner closed over them than it seemed to be sucked away from their bodies, to curve upwards at their feet, to arch over their heads, until it formed a perfect spheroid.' I descend the stairs without incident, no child, green or of any other colour, to lead me.

Men and women change in unisex rooms in France. A friend who played water polo for Australia and is a masters swimming champ tells me this convention dates from the days when only men swam in Europe. Athletic swimming, as opposed to genteel breast-stroking, was seen to be unfeminine. It's only recently, he believes, that women *en masse* dipped their toes in the water. There are cubicles you can lock, I hasten to add, but showers and most wet areas are common to the genders. I suspect that this thrills many men who aren't used to it and probably appalls many women. At this pool, you get a kind of clothes-horse or dumb-butler in blue plastic for your belongings and give it to an attendant in return for a numbered rubber bracelet that most swimmers wear around their ankles.

The pool is a standard twenty-five metres long and has about eight lanes. All but two are being used for coaching or mucking about in. None of the lap lanes is marked fast, medium or slow, and swimmers of various speeds (there are nine in the lane I choose) are trudging — or its aqueous equivalent — up and down, reluctantly exercising, it seems. I swim a few laps with difficulty because of the crowd. A middle-aged bloke with the body of a skinned rabbit has a no beg-pardons approach. He's ripping up and down, overtaking when he shouldn't, raining accidental blows on others with an extravagant crawl. Even on those swimming in the same direction. He shows utter contempt for people going the other way. He collides and ploughs on. His *bonnet de bain* (swimming cap) is stamped in block letters RCF — Racing Club de France, I guess, which is a very snobbish and exclusive organisation. He must be a member, I reason, begrudging having to train with the hoi-poloi. I take off after him, catch him, and clip him firmly on the heels with my hand. I do it again. I don't like him, he doesn't like me, but I think he gets the message. He glares at me as we turn, but I detect a little more deference from then on.

A girl in a very slinky and virtually transparent red one-piece stops alongside me at the end of the lane. Her skin is exquisite, pale and smooth, the pool water giving it a high gloss. It's the skin you notice most in Europe, I find. You want to stroke it, a very dubious thing to do, under the circumstances. I struggle to restrain myself. Is it always like this, I ask. (I indicate that I'm talking about the crowding, not her skin. It's my standard opening line in pools.) No, she says, there are usually three lanes. What about signs saying fast, medium and slow? Yes, usually, she says. She doesn't know what's happened today. It wouldn't be the case where I come from, I say.

'England?' she guesses.

'Australia,' I say.

'Oh, well,' she almost sneers, 'you've got more space over there.' She curls a lip and pushes off for the other end.

It's so cold as I walk back to the apartment that the air seems to be crystallising, turning into a brittle icy mist all by itself. I shower and change and, when I rejoin the rue des Petites Ecuries, rugged up, scarved, gloved and wearing an old woollen ski beanie, snow is falling very lightly.

I'm off first to the big shops, as they call them — the department stores on boulevard Haussmann. I want to revisit a favourite place, the food hall of Galeries Lafayette. By the time I get to the Folies Bergère, four hundred metres from my front door, the snow is heavy. There is virtually no wind and flakes the size of rose petals waft down, swinging like pendulums as they descend. The Folies these days, by the way, remains an important music hall where many acts — from jazz performers to risqué reviews — are staged. A plaque outside, though, boasts of its hottest and most glorious days in the 1920s: of Josephine Baker, who made her name here in 1926 wearing a belt made of bananas; Colette, who gave women riding instructions on ball-breaking many decades before the liberation of her gender was a twinkle in Germaine's brain; and Maurice Chevalier, the vaudevillian boulevardier without peer. I photograph the gorgeous art-deco façade and its nude dancer, who seems to be ascending into the clouds or perhaps walking on water across a stream. Braving increasingly heavy snow, which is by now gathering on windscreen wipers and the seats of scooters parked on footpaths, I take a left at the rue Laffitte then a right onto the boulevard. In ten minutes I'm up the escalator and at the entrance to the food hall.

It's always busy — in fact, the whole store is always busy. Today, a few weeks from Christmas, even more people crowd in. Perhaps they're sheltering from the snow. I unpack myself, removing gloves, beanie and scarf. I get my camera out and snap stacks of gift boxes containing teas and spices. Indeed, there are dozens of loose spices in bright tin buckets tiered around the stairwell.

As I frame my second shot I feel a gentle tap on my left arm. In a grey suit and tie, a smiling north African fellow apologises for having to tell me that photos are not allowed. I tell him what I'm doing — the photos will be needed for my notes. Galeries Lafayette will get terrific publicity. He's sorry, he says, but any photography has to be cleared by management. I suggest he gets on the walkie-talkie he's carrying and arranges permission. He agrees, walks away from me, pushes buttons and puts the device to his ear. I look around for potential shots. There are many in the distance beyond the very wide entrance. The security chap returns after a couple of minutes. He can't get authorisation quickly, he says. I must get it in writing. In fact, I should have *got* it in writing weeks ago. I didn't know, I say, and I've got to take photographs today. He moves away again and stabs buttons. A minute later he's back. Perhaps a few photos only, he says. Two or three, he suggests. I up the ante. What about ten? No, not ten, he says. Eight? He shakes his head, smiles broadly and walks away. I interpret this move as permission for restrained open slather. Who's going to count? I stride across the polished granite tiles of Lafayette Gourmet and bang away.

There might be bigger and better and more exclusive food shops in the world, but Lafayette suits me. In refrigerated cabinets behind spotless curved glass fronts is just about anything you might ever want to eat, including the most expensive. No man might be an island, but each speciality here has its own octagonal island. There's Vidal duck foie gras, fig chutney, caramelised onions, chicken and *confit* onions that you're meant to use in a couscous, lamb and onion confit, and goose foie gras made by Castaing and priced at a very reasonable 65.50 euros for 325 grams.

And after just about every snap of the shutter a server tells me I can't take pictures. This is fine the first five times. I tell them all — to the last white-coated, blue-aproned, flat-capped, hairnetted man and women — that I've been given permission. But about the sixth time I get a little exasperated. (I shouldn't have, I know.) I tell the young bloke in the cheese octagon, his cap the shape of flatbread, that I'm probably the most important food writer in the entire world and if he lets me take his picture he might become very famous and I might get my job done quicker. No photos, he says, holding up his hand like a Hollywood star. Mind you, my monologue also has the desired effect of his running a mile from the lens.

Hundreds of cheeses are there, including many raw-milk confections at risible prices — fresh goats'-milk cheeses, for instance, at 2 to 3 euros for a whole small cylinder. Scottish smoked salmon costs 100 euros the kilo, with smoked eel at 10 euros a kilo less. The famous fabricant Dalloyau has many lines on display, including Norwegian egg, which is capped with smoked salmon, for 9 euros the piece; perfect transparent dark-brown obelisks of *pot au feu* (a type of beef stew) in jelly for 6.60 euros; and eggs in jelly containing slivers of zucchini and carrot for 3 euros. Dalloyau's chocolate and petits fours have made its name, though, and there is quite a range of loose flat choc-blocks of various strengths at high prices. A 375–gram box of Dalloyau's best assorteds will set you back 34.50 euros. And everywhere I look money is changing hands.

A side aisle leads to Lafayette Gourmet's wine shop, where there is excellent buying. But in such an important firm as this one, in such an esteemed gastronomic site as this, nonsense in English welcomes the anglophone. A notice says:

> '*Wine a world of buffs and enthusiasts, appeals to the tide senses. And more besides LAFAYETTE GOURMET work together with Winegrowers who are keen to express their region.*
>
> *Like a publisher urging his authors on to produce their best work we have put together this collection to help you build up your own to your personal taste.*'

Love the publisher and authors stuff.

Outside, the snow is falling more heavily, gathering centimetres thick on the roofs of parked cars. The crowds are heavy along the footpath, many of them parents showing children the fairly dowdy Christmas displays in the department-store windows. I scamper to a Métro entrance to take line eight to La Motte Picquet Grenelle.

I'm heading home, or the precinct of Paris I once called home. In the Métro, I listen for the long tenor note the undercarriage makes between Invalides and La Tour-Maubourg. The trains go around slow dark curves, and an air on a rail prevails. It's accompanied by a chorus of squeaks, metal on metal. And has been for as long as I can remember. Brakes, possibly? The sounds are all very comforting. Like grunts, they indicate to me that one of the most efficient and easy to use transport systems in a big city is going about its daily routine in a businesslike manner.

The temperature descends abruptly as I arise from the tunnels into the avenue de la Motte Picquet. Right outside where I want to go, as it happens — I've picked the correct exit for a change. In this corner café-brasserie, Le Bouquet de Grenelle, I met with a few friends the night before my wedding. We got very drunk. I can't recall patronising it at other times in the 1970s and I don't feel like going in today. I do have enormous sympathy, though, for the stout, rubber-aproned fellow outside the cafe selling Normandy oysters under his scarlet-and-yellow awning. Snow is falling as if the world's doonas have burst. I turn right and head up the boulevard towards the river.

Rather than changing lines here for the single-stop journey to Dupleix on the elevated grey viaduct in cross-hatched steel, I often used to walk. It seemed a much longer hike after work in the 1970s than it does today. But, then again, it's not midnight, and I haven't finished nine exhausting hours rewriting French despatches about hostages and Middle-Eastern madness — terrorists at Munich and the attacks that followed. I haven't sprinted numerous times across a crowded room with a flash about bodies and *attentats* and Palestinians and Israelis. I haven't returned home as tired as a coalminer and covered in carbon. In those pre-tech days only representatives of two *métiers* came home black after work: miners and agency journalists. We had typewriters then, and everything was done in carbon triplicate.

I pass the little shop where a wizened old chap used to fix radios. His horn-framed spectacles seemed larger than his face. He was learning to repair television sets, he told me one day when I picked up our radio. Black-and-white, of course. The shop's windows are papered over, and I guess that, long ago, it lost its sign — Valdiv, was it, or Valdez radio repairs? So many businesses along this stretch of road seem to be in commercial limbo. So many shops have their windows blanked. I can't explain it. I pass the corner restaurant where I took my parents on their first night in Paris. It's a real-estate agency. Then I take the slight bend in the road — pavements are getting slippery as the snow freezes and traffic is moving at snail's pace — past the Dupleix station. ('Dupleix', by the way, is pronounced 'duplex', not 'duplay'. French proper names are usually sounded out, especially Breton-sounding ones such as Dupleix. In general, French make no attempt to obliterate the consonants in names.) A little way farther on and I'm at number one rue Clodion, my home for three years.

Poilâne, the famous bread shop, is still on the corner. It was the second in the Poilâne empire, opening just before I came to live over it. Pierre Poilâne started his first bakery in 1932 in the rue du Cherche Midi, the sixth arrondissement. But in the post-war years he objected to white industrial bread and rode a tide of increasing affluence with his artisan sourdough loaves. By 1970 his son Lionel had taken over.

The shop remains as it was when I lived above it. On the wall beside its facing of narrow brown bricks is a bas-relief of a windmill. About seven or eight metres below our bed, Poilâne's ovens warmed the whole building all night. It was great in winter. We were never cold. But I never liked Poilâne's bread, even if it was produced from wild yeasts and stone-ground wholewheat flour, baked in wood-fired ovens and seasoned with Guérande salt.

Today I buy my favourite Poilâne offerings: a little *chausson aux pommes* and a small button-shaped roll. I met Lionel Poilâne once in Australia and told him where I had lived. He seemed a little tetchy and uninterested, although his entourage gave me a cushion shaped like one of his loaves.

These days a couple of dozen ovens and forty bakers daily produce thousands of loaves that are dispersed to hundreds of shops and restaurants throughout Paris and overseas. In 2002, Lionel Poilâne, his wife and their dog died when the helicopter he was piloting went into the sea off Brittany. They were heading for their holiday home on a small island. Today the *chausson* is excellent, its pastry so flaky and light, its filling of apple purée magnificent, tasty and lightly nutmegged. I eat it and the roll looking up at my former windows and little balcony. What great days we had in that tiny studio, even if you needed to climb over the stove to get to the shower. I regret never having taken many photographs.

I cross under the viaduct, where the pigeon droppings are thick and a street market operates, but not today, and take the rue de Lourmel, which has a tradition of good food shops. In its first fifty metres off the boulevard there is a champion cheese outlet, a *patisserie*, a great fish shop, a butcher and a couple of *charcuteries*. This is the fifteenth, too — locals have money and they are very white and old French. The difference in appearance between a cluster of Parisians here and a similar-sized group where I'm living north of the river is striking. The people of the fifteenth are homogeneously *bourgeois*. At selected shops, they are queueing in the street. In the snow. Now, it's true that some of them might be standing and waiting because a particular shop has become fashionable — in the way that Poilâne caught the imagination of Parisian consumers in the 1970s. But there will be enough standing in line who know their tucker to make it worth your while wrapping up and getting behind them. You might have a bit of a wait on your hands, but what you buy and eat at the end of the line will be excellent. These are neither Russian bread queues nor African humanitarian grain lines. They might best be described as Gallic gourmet queues.

I retrace my steps in the snow — some of it is mounding under doorsteps and by buildings now. It falls constantly, the

sky from which it's coming the dullest grey imaginable. The
buildings seem morose, and the few pedestrians about are so
enveloped in what they are wearing that they appear barely
human. I take the avenue de la Motte Picquet towards the
Champs de Mars. It's a broad thoroughfare with classy shops
and a few stylish brasseries. There's a memorable view coming
up. With your back to the Ecole Militaire, you look up the
Champs to the Eiffel Tower. But I'm unprepared for the sight
today. The wide formal gardens and alleys are blanketed in
snow. It's Siberian. The top of the Eiffel Tower is in cloud. I
have never before seen Paris like this.

I get out my camera and snap away. Quite by accident,
one image shows two couples and two people quite distant
from each other. But what's astonishing about it is the perfect
chevron they make to a vanishing point on the horizon. They
mimic the triangle of the tower itself and the perspective of the
alleys against the white of the snow. At the bottom right a male
has just entered the frame, and in the far left someone weighed
down by bags — it's impossible to distinguish gender — is
bent over atrociously and appears to be limping. One couple
cross in the middle distance, and the second couple, a little
closer, are taking photos with a tripod. Henri Cartier-Bresson
would have 'seen' this shot. I certainly didn't. He believed the
best photographers *saw* the magical visual instants that most
of us miss. Moreover, they were quick enough with their index
fingers to capture them. I smile, realising I've had an
accidental Cartier-Bresson moment.

In the foreground is the Peace Wall, a monument of
glass, steel and wood installed in 2000. It was supposed to be
removed to the UNESCO headquarters after three months
but is still here. It's essentially two enormous glass panels in
which 'peace' is engraved in thirty-two languages and thirteen
alphabets. Thin columns repeatedly spell out the word, and a
boardwalk links it all. A few tourists dawdle about. In the
superstructure's niches are video screens on which you are

invited to leave a message for the world. A mischievous thought crosses my mind. I struggle to remove gloves and put on my glasses. I can't get the videoscreen to work. Just as well. I was tempted to write that while humans exist wars will be waged. That fighting is in their blood. Man is a vicious, competitive bastard by nature. Greedy by nature, too. But in the aftermath of wars birthrates are excellent, something several Western governments would love to have right now. Economies are rebuilt and become stronger and fairer after wars — see those of Germany and Japan. Whole countries are sometimes rebuilt to be more democratic and resilient — see Vietnam. The technical innovations that have far-reaching effects in peacetime — see radar and other electronic sensing, computing and rocketry, to name a few — are often developed only because of the imperatives of war. I hate war as much as anyone, but wars usually produce benefits for vast numbers of people. That's what I would have written. But I hardly think that these thoughts would be welcome on the Peace Wall.

<hr />

I'm trying another high recommendation for dinner: ze kitchen galerie, in fashionable lower-case letters, is said to be doing new things for Paris, using Thai flavours. It's not far from Fogón, so I don't need to tell you what I'm thinking as I approach along the quai des Grands Augustins.

How swish and contemporary — so like new brasseries in Melbourne. Although to be fair to my home town, most of them provide comfortable chairs these days. I've been on about uncomfortable seating in restaurants for decades. The galerie's chairs score half-marks. The seats are spacious and upholstered in red fabric, but the armrests are narrow and tubular — hopeless. The chairs are also too diverting *per se*. Any chair that makes you look at it can't be good to sit upon. It's a general rule, and I'll leave you to find the exceptions. Luckily, I've got my length of bench seating against a wall.

The galerie is medium-sized. Its floor is of unvarnished pine strips, and narrow Pollock-type canvases in black and vivid reds and yellows hang on white walls. (I remember Clement Greenberg, who discovered Jackson, once told me that every splodge the artist made was intentional to the millimetre. Yeah, Clem, yeah.) Cooks in a small exposed kitchen slave away in the back corner.

Froths, croquettes and salt are *à la mode* in Paris. It seems you have to have them pretty liberally to be a successful restaurant. It's what I'll remember most about ze kitchen galerie, at any rate. None of the dishes is magical. There's an attempt, at least, I tell myself, to use lemongrass, ginger and chilli. But it's not right: half-hearted and out of balance. Are the chefs afraid of overdoing things, frightening away customers with conservative Gallic palates? No dish lights up.

I've asked for a dégustation, and I'm tasting a handful of fairly small offerings. There have been a couple of chunks of tuna with a vinaigrette, half-moons of black and red radish, and a salty prawn mince. A crustacean soup is pretty one-dimensional with lemongrass and nori shreds. Prawn tails have a lively crunchiness. A couple of bream ravioli have good strong fishiness but are a little too salty — alarm bells ring! They're said to be flavoured with Thai herbs but I can't detect the references. Topped with nori and chives, they're in a green cress froth with a medicinal flavour. Using herbs in contemporary French cooking often seems to result in tastes achieved by infusing a sachet in water to sleep well. Sometimes, some herbal concoctions taste as if they should be smoked. Or taken for an ailment. (Like the rest of the West, the French are obsessed with herbal cures. Shelves upon shelves of pills and capsules that can redress any physiological imbalance known to man are sold each day.) But, to my mind, medicine is not gastronomy. That zinging freshness that Australian cooks have extracted by gentrifing plants of the south-east Asian floodlands is missing.

The galerie's platings are very attractive — worth the covers of food glossies. It's unusual for dishes to look good in French restaurants, and on this score alone this place deserves loud applause. A *croquette* of hare and foie gras is OK but hardly distinguished. Mealy and chewy, it's accompanied by a chilled fruit purée that is equally ordinary. Beetroot purée sits between two slices of root and some black trumpet mushrooms garnish. I describe a fawn sauce on the plate in my notebook as 'obscure', meaning that its flavour doesn't leap out and grab you. But at least it *has* flavour — based on hare stock, I'd guess — and has come to the table unaerated. The galerie's entrées cost 13 to 14 euros, with mains mostly priced between 23 and 30 euros.

On the way out, I suggest to one of the very young front-of-house team that the cooks ought to go to London and try the food of David Thompson at Nahm. Have a look at what the former Sydney boy, the world's leading Thai high cook, is doing. For fifteen years, his versions of regal Siamese dishes and his originality with what are said to be the classic Thai ingredients (in recent years they have been incorporated into many other indigenous cooking styles, of course) have been peerless. The young chap looks vague.

'David *qui*?' he asks.

# day seven

Sunday morning, and I have a family lunch ahead: I've been invited by my brother-in-law and his wife. It'll be a real Gallic Sunday lunch, which can be everything special and nothing special, in French terms, depending on who is attending and whether any celebrations are in order. It is, however, *always* good and substantial, a serious meal with which to start the week. But neither their son nor daughter will be coming, so sitting down will be just Josiane, Jean-Pierre and me.

They live in the eastern suburban fringes about seventeen kilometres from the centre of Paris. And, while you can zip around the city itself fairly quickly, once you leave the centre for farther points, commuting can take time. Where they live is not all that easy to get to, even if two fast-train lines (RERs) run fairly close by. So getting near is relatively easy, but the last three or four kilometres, through narrow streets that were pioneered by haycarts centuries ago, tend to snare the big teal-blue Renault buses. And from the bus stop you must walk about five hundred metres.

Jean-Pierre and Josiane moved here in the early 1970s because the place lacked a good butchery. He retired recently, a man of considerable means. His modern home, with its vast living areas paved in polished stone, sits in generous gardens. Towering over the lawns are conifers, an enormous walnut tree, and plum and apple trees of various species. There are roses and rhododendrons, and a new BMW in the double garage.

I love visiting them. We talk a lot about food and cooking, where the French are going gastronomically (often not a happy discussion), politics and taxes. We almost never talk about restaurants because, like many French, Josiane and Jean-Pierre dine out very rarely. Sometimes they will admit that they've been disappointed. Josiane cooks sublimely, and her meals are built from the ground up, from the raw materials. And, as we eat, Jean-Pierre regales the gathered with spontaneous puns and word-plays, his eyes glistening with fun. I've never noted a single one, they erupt so instinctively. And they're mostly very clever. They flash and die, but within a minute or so another bursts from his lips. Life has hurled some very nasty vicissitudes at Jean-Pierre and Josiane, yet they both remain charming, generous, modest and high-hearted. I enjoy being with them enormously — so much, in fact, that to go there partly to work (the situation today) is a little dispiriting.

I change from the Métro to RER line A at Châtelet les Halles, get off at Noisy-le-Grand, find the right exit for the bus station in the enormous commercial centre constructed above the rails, and take the bus, which is full of French Africans from north and south. With waiting time it's a ninety-minute journey on a Sunday.

As always, the welcome is *chaleureux*. I've brought a bottle of bordeaux, for which I paid a little more than average. When I first came to France, *invités* took a pot of flowers or a fruit tart to their hosts. Increasingly, you can offer a good bottle. Within about ten minutes — these people speak at formula-one pace — we're all up-to-speed with recent family events, jobs and the amount our adult children are paying in rent. (Nothing when they're at home, which is both wonderful and lamentable for their parents.) Small triumphs are announced and, happily, only a few smaller tragedies are revealed. We decide, as we agree tacitly every time, that the world is in equal measure atrocious and wonderful. None of us, if I remember rightly, has ever tried to explain why. We just say that it's like that, a common expression.

The table is set, white plates with gold rims dressing an elegant cloth worked with yellow and navy daisies. Stemmed wine glasses and horn-handled cutlery wait to be used. Luxurious floral napkins that match the tablecloth are at hand, and three rustic chairs with seats of woven rushes are ready to be pulled out and sat upon. Josiane tells me several times that we're having a simple lunch — she has gone to no trouble. A tall, elegant and attractive blonde, she appears at least ten years younger than her age. Jean-Pierre, who is a few years over sixty, has slightly thinning brushed-back hair. Only in the past couple of years has it shown a light seasoning of more salt than pepper. Solid, he is shorter than three of his seven sisters.

Over many years, the family has listened with infinite patience to my talk of Australian cooking and restaurants. Not once do I remember either Josiane or Jean-Pierre insisting that the French way was best. Or that what I claim about the freshness and originality of Australian cooking can't be right. We drink a bottle of champagne, an habitual aperitif in French middle-class families, even if there is nothing special to celebrate. Jean-Pierre warms up with a little word-play about the *boules* (bubbles) in the *coupe* (champagne glass) and the *coupes* (winners' cups) in *boules* (otherwise known as *pétanque*, the bowls game played with heavy iron spheres and a jack). And we sit down to lunch.

It's simple, says Josiane again, as she places a large oval platter of tomato slices in the middle of the table. Jean-Pierre pops the cork out of a dry white wine from his region, the Loire. Dressed in a vinaigrette sauce and topped with chopped chives and shallots, the tomato slices are a deep-scarlet and oozing juice into the barely whisked oil and acid. They are delicious and full-flavoured. He's had a lot of success this year with his tomatoes, says Jean-Pierre. These are the very last of the season, picked in the week before I arrived. It was mild, he says, then the cold arrived. Very quickly. They're called beef's hearts. I should be very clear, he smiles, that they are from the beef's *coeur* (heart) and not his *queue* (tail). Do I want him to write that down? I retort with a laugh, knowing that he knows that I know the different sounds these two words make, even if some English-speakers might find them difficult to tell apart.

Next up are mussels from the Mont-Saint-Michel bay in Normandy. They're famously known as *moules de bouchon*, which needs some explaining. *Moules* are mussels, of course, and a *bouchon* amounts to rank upon rank of vertical sticks stuck in shallow tidal water. Mussels attach themselves and grow on the sticks. You might have seen images of *bouchons* — pickets protruding from the sea by half an arm's length — stretching to infinity. And you will certainly have seen photographs of Mont-Saint-Michel, exposed tidal flats all around, such are the sea surges in this part of the world. *Bouchon* mussels are small — about the size of half a thumb — and Josiane has cooked them quickly and classically in white wine with onions and a sprig of thyme. Parsley choppings speckle them. And they're excellent — their flesh firm, its colour a dark orange-saffron. An argument goes that small bivalves taste better than bigger ones, but I point out that the much larger blue mussels (about four times the volume of the Normandy mussels) grown in Victoria's Port Phillip Bay are more delicately gelatinous but retain very good flavour. And that even more spectacular are the huge Spring Bay mussels (twice the size of the Port Phillip variety) cultivated in 'lanterns' of plastic mesh in the cold and spectacularly clean (and nutritious) waters off the east coast of Tasmania. These observations are greeted with interest.

For main course we have something of the highest quality, says Jean-Pierre. Roasted lamb shoulder, but not just any lamb. This is Elovel lamb from the Lozère in south central France, a plateau of 1000 metres altitude. It's the best time to be eating it, too. The ewes and lambs are free-ranging, and at the end of autumn indigenous herbs and grasses are most highly flavoured. Jean-Pierre dashes off to get printed information for me. From the kitchen, I hear sizzling. He returns with a thick file in tanned leather, newspaper clippings and press releases catalogued within it, each with its own plastic sleeve. The lamb's race is Massif Central white. They eat such plants as *mélilot*, bush cumin, *pimprenelle*, box and angel's hair. After a hundred days, they're taken from their mothers and have to forage. Cereals supplement their diets, and by the time they're slaughtered they weigh about thirty kilos and have been alive just a few months. Their health is monitored throughout, and the birth certificates with which the best beasts are sold double as death certificates. The controlling authority *Agneaux de Lozère* (Lozère lambs) recommends that they're consumed eight days after killing. I ask Jean-Pierre how much they retail for. He lifts his head, reflects, and says about 14 to15 euros a kilo.

Josiane returns with the shoulder in slices on a platter and an accompanying boat containing the reduced cooking juices. They've been emulsified with butter, she says. And how does she roast the lamb, I ask. Like a *rappeur*, says Jean-Pierre. Hot and short. I detect that the smile she sends her husband is somewhat forced. '*Effectivement*,' she says politely. The shoulder is trussed, of course, and put in a roasting dish with roughly chopped garlic, a dried bay leaf, some water and sunflower oil. She puts knobs of butter on top of the joint and adds dried rosemary. Her oven is very hot, she adds — about 250 degrees Celsius — and she roasts the meat for about forty minutes, basting every now and then. Like most roasts you will eat in France, quite a lot of the meat at the centre of the joint will be uncooked, warm-raw. This one is done a little more than usual — perhaps because I'm here. It's astonishing, at any rate, the best lamb I've eaten. It's not so much the complex sweetness of the meat that is so wonderful, it's the texture — the grain of the muscle is so fine, rawer parts almost like red-raw tuna. We have standard green beans fried in butter and garlic to accompany. (And a burgundy Jean-Pierre thinks might go well with the lamb.) Thin young green beans are getting difficult to find, says Josiane. Increasingly they're imported from Africa; Senegalese are the best, but she also buys Kenyan and Moroccan beans. Until fairly recently you could easily buy beans grown in France. These days they are rare and expensive — it's becoming too dear to harvest them by hand when they are only half a centimetre in diameter. The French won't do it, and, increasingly, immigrants won't either, Jean-Pierre says. African beans are cheaper.

We eat a salad of *endives* — which are known as witlof in some countries — containing pieces of the couple's own walnuts, followed by a platter of cheeses, including a brie from Meaux, a fresh goat's cheese and a roquefort. All are made from raw (unpasteurised) milk (the roquefort from ewe's milk) and have brilliant complexity and depth of flavour. Every single cheese made from pasteurised milk that attempts to emulate these creations tastes bland. You might as well eat the packaging it comes in. The fakery of big commerce and the exploitation of novice gastronomes is never more blatant than in cheese production. These are real cheeses. Anything less is rubbish.

And I tell Jean-Pierre that, once again, we've come to the end of the meal without noting enough of the funny things he has said. I've been enjoying myself too much, I say. Can he remember anything? '*Eh ben...*' he says — a colloquial 'Well'. He furrows his brow between guffaws. Nothing, he says. I'll bring a digicorder next time, I say menacingly. After strong black coffee and a promise from me to pass on their love to Jean-Pierre's two sisters in Australia, they drive me to Noisy and the RER. Kisses all round.

By late evening, I'm ready to try another Bib Gourmand, especially after the success of the Pré Cadet. Buisson Ardent is in the fifth, the Jussieu quarter, which has a lot of students who attend nearby schools of the university. It's said to be small and has frescoes dating from 1923. I imagine, perhaps unsurprisingly, that it's a bit of a layabouts' hangout — tatty, perhaps, and filled with young people in t-shirts who are so relaxed you could carry them about in buckets. The food will be super-cheap, I tell myself, and not especially good.

Buisson is a complete surprise. It's tiny all right, a walk-in off busy rue Jussieu. But it's modestly elegant, its ceiling high. It's a bit like a palace boudoir. OK, a maidservant's palace boudoir. No oak floor in herringbone pattern, though. Buisson has small, fawn or chocolate-coloured floor tiles and wall-mounted lamps in art-deco style. They depict a bouquet of white lilies, the flowers of smoked pearlescent glass. Heavy brown art paper overlays timber tables and you use alloy cutlery and acceptable glassware. But a real advantage here are huge cream napkins in heavy worked fabric. The walls are panelled in blue and aqua distemper, and they rise to a plaster frieze. And there are indeed frescoes. Autumnal ones, I suppose you could call them. It's the Impressionists' fault — Renoir and Manet especially — for promoting the notion that outdoor leisure in the nineteenth century was idyllic. Romance was exercised in parks and gardens, they argued in oils, and it rubbed off on all kinds of artists well into the twentieth century.

Although they were conceived and created at a time when Paris vied with Berlin to be Europe's most amoral city, when mobsters ruled in Chicago and German politics was about to gamble on a monster, Buisson's wall stories are peaceful, bucolic and charming. A full moon rises behind a mill. Two sheep graze in lush grass beside a winding metre-wide brook. Another panel, another mill (this time powered by wind) and the scene is wintry, snow deep. A nearby lake appears to be frozen. But two panels of lovers are the most arresting. (Buisson's painters, by the way, were of no more than modest talent, in my view.) Perhaps they are the same couple; it's hard to tell. In the first, they are chastely kissing in a nineteenth-century manner as they cross a bridge in a town. The second is tragic, its heartbreak enacted in a formal French garden on steps: an urn at the top of a heavy stone balustrade tumbles with pink geraniums; the young woman stands at the top of the flight, her body yearning towards her lover, two steps down. Her right arm is outstretched and he's kissing her hand with a look of resignation. These things must be, says his body language. She is devastated, and he is probably a cad.

Buisson offers gastronomic versatility. Starters are listed at 9 euros, mains at 17 euros and desserts at 6 euros — excellent prices for restaurant eating in Paris. But there is also a four-course menu for 35 euros, or 45 euros with wines. The wine list is not extensive, but at least Buisson makes available what are called '*vin de pays*', or modest regional wines, at pretty low prices. Two are on special tonight at 19 euros the bottle, and a 2004 red made from grenache and shiraz grapes in the Duché d'Uzes in the south-west is quite acceptable.

I select the menu, beginning with two thin ovals of foie gras said to be cooked with red wine. Not a plating would grace any magazine cover, it puts the fattened liver to the south, strings of balsamic-sweated onion to the north-east and centimetre cubes of mango to the north-west. Balsamic vinegar is terribly chic. It shouldn't be, in my view. Few chefs restrain it. It needs to be buckled, employed to give the faintest of medicinal accents. Cough-mixture flavours. The onion, said on the menu to be a '*confiture*', is spoiled by the balsamic, at any rate. The cold foie gras terrine itself is fine, and the mango, said to be a chutney, is more or less just mango.

Cumin is another flavour that's popular in France. Again, I find it has to be treated with care. This time, though, it's well-handled, a nice scent in a central pile of strings of carrot and zucchini. Three scallops in a well-balanced, sour burnt-butter sauce surround the vegies, and the bivalves themselves are springy, tasty and quite sweet. I like it, even if, once again, it is fairly rudimentary on the visual side.

Tables fill. There are couples, young and old. A family celebration of some sort sees three generations take eight seats. The Buisson packs customers in fairly closely, and before long I'm overhearing a couple restraining themselves to my left. They're bursting to hammer and tong one another — '*Tu as le droit?*' ('You have the right?') the wife snaps indignantly at one point — and I'm delighted there's a restaurant between us. I turn off when the husband begins telling his wife that she must try to understand, although I'm all for communication and understanding.

Dish number three is half a stuffed quail presented on shreds of sweated cabbage. Surrounding the lot is a fine brown juice built, it's obvious, from an excellent poultry stock. The stuffing is barely OK, though, and it's too salty. And the little bird — these days they're bred for the table — is very small, its flesh scant. It's a jockey of a quail, quite disappointing alongside even the smallest of the species I've been served elsewhere. But I finish with a wonderful dish — a slice of terrifically powerful chocolate terrine as dense and rich as a Brazilian striker, and a wonderful *mousse au chocolat* in a pot. A lot of chocolate dust has blown in all over the plate — from a chocolate desert — and there are also chocolate dribbles and almond shavings. I can't help thinking that, for a country where elegance is prized, it seldom makes it onto restaurant plates.

I'm not too far from the world's most famous English-language bookshop, Shakespeare & Company, which is open from noon to midnight, seven days a week. Its address in the rue de la Bûcherie dates from 1951, when it was opened by a young American, George Whitman, who was studying French at the Sorbonne. (A *bûcherie* has nothing to do with meat, by the way — it's a woodyard.) Writers Henry Miller, Lawrence Durrell and Alan Ginsberg, among many, sought sanctuary, quiet, reading space and talk here.

But let's not confuse the present shop with the original Shakespeare & Company, which Sylvia Beach, a refugee from stifling American Protestantism (she has my sympathy), opened in 1912. Its first address was in the rue Dupuytren; its second and most famous at 12 rue de l'Odéon. On its website, the present Shakespeare & Company says it has continued Sylvia Beach's legacy. Some legacy! It was to the rue de l'Odéon in April 1921 that James Joyce went to seek consolation after another knockback for his gigantic novel *Ulysses*. 'My book will never come out now,' Joyce's biographer, Richard Ellmann, quotes him as saying. And Sylvia said, 'Would you let Shakespeare & Company have the honour of bringing out your *Ulysses*?' The following year, the greatest twentieth-century English novel appeared. (And wouldn't we all love to own one of those first thousand copies?) Hemingway borrowed books from Shakespeare & Company because he had no money to buy them. Sylvia, he wrote, 'had pretty legs and she was kind, cheerful and interested... No-one I ever knew was nicer to me.'

In style and content, the present Shakespeare & Company must be similar to the original. I enter a small front room straight off the street, then realise the place is a warren of nooks and crannies, couches, cushions and cats. The colour of every single well-worn bookshop in the world is brown. (At least bookshops used to be brown, in the days when they sold reading rather than envy.) This place seems browner. It's dusty and musty and every square centimetre of wall is shelved with books. There are tables supporting stacks of books. Some books are new and some are old. Prices vary erratically. At ten o'clock at night perhaps a dozen people graze intellectually.

Up the steepest and most dangerous staircase in France is a second floor of more crannies, nooks and books. Turn a corner, and you'll discover a low velveted divan on which lounges a surly student stroking a purring tortoiseshell. The second-floor books are not for sale, but you may use them for private research. From my overhearing, it seems that most of the customers are young and French. The only person making any real noise is the manager, an American in his early twenties wearing a chocolate corduroy jacket and a wispy goatie. He is being petulant — in English — for anyone who cares to listen. In particular, he is objecting to a cookbook that gives weights in pounds and ounces. 'What sort of a cookbook is this?' he exclaims, throwing it down. He is also performing, it seems to me, for an attractive, large Asian girl who has come in seeking work.

I buy *The Return of Sherlock Holmes*, a Penguin paperback, for 11 euros, just for the fun of it, and he stamps its title page with 'Sylvia Beach Whitman Foundation' under 'Shakespeare & Company'. Also, 'Kilometer Zero Paris', whatever that might mean. He takes off on a new tack. 'What's the French for porpoise?' he screams to nobody in particular. The Asian girl looks nonplussed. Three or four browsers are uninterested. I head for the exit and, with the door half-open, turn to him and suggest that the word is '*dauphin*'.

'No,' he snaps at me. 'That's a dolphin. I want porpoise! Porpoise! What's the French for porpoise?'

I leave, suspecting that *Ulysses* would fail to get published these days.

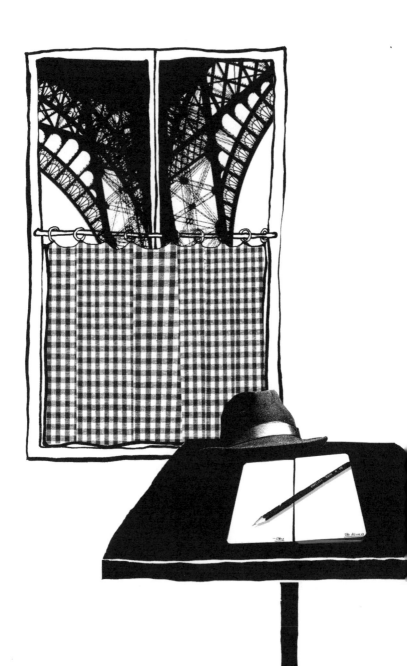

# day eight

Owing to a bureaucratic oversight, as most fuck-ups are called these days, I'm having to change apartments this morning. As the crow flies, my next abode is only about a kilometre away. But I'm not walking it with a backpack, daypack, computer and paraphernalia. Actually it's a toss-up. Let's say I *would* walk a little over a kilometre to reach the new place. Not a huge hike at all. If I take the Métro, I'll have to descend and then climb a series of stairs and escalators when I change at Barbès Rochechouart for the overhead line heading west towards Pigalle. But in a relatively flat city, heading north from the rue des Petites Ecuries means climbing steadily uphill once I get into the rue de Rochechouart. So it's a toss-up. I clean up the studio, remember my camembert in the fridge — it has been maturing nicely, I can feel — and give Monsieur Montebello's room a final longing glance. And I take the Métro.

They know I'm coming, I tell myself, and it's ten o'clock, when every concierge in Paris is sorting keys, sweeping corridors, or bringing in the bins. I'll just pick up my key to the new place, let myself in and relax a little before lunch at the Eiffel Tower.

The ascent from line four to line two at Barbès is easier than I expected and I even have a seat for part of the four-station journey. I get out at Anvers, walk back down the boulevard and take a left into the narrow rue Seveste. It rises gently to the grassy square Willette, just beneath Sacré-Coeur. The massive oak door to number sixteen, a building of several stories, is only a score or so metres from the park and a merry-go-round. The funicular railway that takes you up the hill to Sacré-Coeur is a little further on.

Madame Galena, who owns the apartment, has sent me the digicodes for the outside and inside doors and I struggle through them. A short dark corridor leads to a small interior courtyard paved in concrete. It's about the size of a very large prison cell, and I feel condemned almost immediately. Opposite the corridor are windows hung with lace curtains, obviously the concierge's apartment. No lights are on and nobody is about. I peer through the windows. A table with family photographs is barely visible in the gloom. I am to deal directly with Madame Fernandez, Madame Galena has told me. I knock for the third time. No answer. Nobody. Not a soul comes or goes. And it's very cold, only slightly warmer here than in the street.

Parisian concierges are almost never away from their posts. And there'd be a Monsieur Fernandez, too, and he is also absent. They can't be away for long, I tell myself. An elderly gent in a cloth cap emerges from one of two winding staircases that empty into the courtyard. Does he know where Madame Fernandez might be? Isn't she here, he says with surprise. She's always here, he adds. Perhaps she's just slipped out to the shops. He offers to try to find her or her husband in the *quartier*. He'll send one of them back to let me in.

I wait. Soon it's eleven and I'm getting cold. A woman in her thirties comes down the second staircase. Madame Fernandez does cleaning at the pharmacy nearby, she says.

Perhaps she's there. I leave my gear, go back outside and look up and down the street. Several shops sell bolts of coloured fabrics, but I can't see a pharmacy. I return to the courtyard and ring the agency. Oh, Monsieur Downes, what bad luck. But you should have made an appointment to tell the concierge when you were arriving. She knew I was arriving, I say to Wolfgang, who has handled my bookings. He sounds German and insists on speaking English. 'Did I have to give an hour?' I say, a little tetchily. He will get on the phone immediately, he says, and ring me back.

Ten more minutes pass before my phone rings. The owner's daughter is coming in from the suburbs to let me in, he says. 'Where is she now?' I ask. In the suburbs coming in to Paris — not far, is all he can offer. Doesn't *he* have keys? No, he says. Now, I have a fair idea of what coming in from Parisian suburbs can mean. A two-hour wait? Ninety minutes if I'm lucky? Nothing else can be done, because Madame Galena herself is in Italy, says Wolfgang. 'Oh!' I say.

Twenty minutes pass and I ring the agency again. Look, I say, I have work to do and can't wait for either the concierge or the owner's daughter. Can he please hurry them up? Wolfgang says he'll see what he can do. A quarter-hour passes and I get another call. A woman's voice shrieks through a cacophony of traffic and bursts of laughter. Her voice is breaking up, too, as if a fixed line somewhere linking us — I know there can't be one — is being repeatedly run over by farting Vespas. I return to the street to listen better. I understand very little. It sounds as if the caller is Madame Galena's daughter. She's ringing from Rome, where she is with her mother. Someone called Michaela, anyway, will let me in. She is coming. I ask when. Perhaps in ten minutes. I thank her for the call.

Wolfgang rings again to apologise, but there is nothing he can do. I tell him I'm leaving my stuff in the courtyard. Madame Fernandez should take it into her apartment for safekeeping when she gets back. Wolfie says he is only the agent. He can't do anything. He must trust owners and concierges to organise such things as the handing over of keys.

I bury the computer in the backpack, take my scant valuables with me and pile the rest of my things outside the concierge's door. On a sheet of A4, I scribble that these are the belongings of Monsieur Downes, who is renting the apartment of Madame Galena. I'll be back before four. Telephone me to tell me how I can get the keys, or leave them in my backpack. Thanks. The Eiffel Tower cannot wait.

Even on this brutally cold morning I'm expecting queues. But I've arrived before lunchtime and shouldn't have to wait long. In fact, there appear to be no lines of tourists at any of the four *piliers* — the bases or feet of the tower. I know enough about Paris's premier tourist site *not* to eat at Le Jules Verne, the tower's one-Michelin-starred restaurant. It's simply the cost. But I go over to the south *pilier* anyway, to read the menu.

It's encased in elegant and substantial glass bordered in gold. 'Jules Verne' is chased in block capitals across the top. The list is in English and among the 'Fishes' is a 'Thick line-fished john dory lightly grilled, duck liver emulsion, pressed potatoes and mushrooms in terrine' for a mere 56 euros. 'Hare from French hunting', as the list puts it, comes in 'two styles, royal style upper part, roasted saddle, potatoes Anna'. Cost? Fifty euros. No, I head directly opposite, crossing the asphalt beneath the tower to the north *pilier*, where ordinary people get in the lifts for the summit and two stops in between. As luck would have it, I'm first in the queue.

My good fortune is ephemeral. It's not my day, obviously. The young woman behind the bank-thick pane of the ticket office waves her hands at me. I can barely understand her. The cluster of tiny holes drilled through the glass between us extrudes our conversation, etiolates it, distorts meaning. The holes are low, too, and I have to bend to make myself heard. Her computer that prints the tickets is broken, she shrugs. I will just have to wait. The wind whips up and others arrive, wrapping themselves as well as they can. At a glance, we might be at the gates of a Siberian gulag.

The queue lengthens. Soon there are forty to fifty people behind me. How long can you wait in France? Piece-of-string time. In the ticket office, personnel lounge around and laugh. It must be warm in there, too, because they're lightly dressed. They smoke. They bellow. Those of us in the queue watch a silent movie. A 'tech' arrives. Must be a 'tech', I reason, because he's wearing a beige pullover and trousers instead of jeans. He dives under the counter, fiddles, and looks at computer screens despairingly, darting from one to another. When an employee comes close to the glass, I shout through the holes, 'Can't you sell tickets by hand?'

'*Non, Monsieur*,' she replies.

I've got time, at least, to decide where I'm going to eat. It will be in the tower's bistro, Altitude 95, on the first level. And how good will it be? I've also got the time to make a bet with myself. The Elior group is a French-listed company with annual revenue of 2.3 billion euros. It has 45,000 employees and 10,600 restaurants and food outlets in Europe and South America. It's the third biggest company in the European food-service market and the biggest provider of food at museums and exhibitions in France. Eliance Restaurants is a branch of the firm. It manages the food outlets at the tower as well as those at the Louvre, the Versailles palace and the Musée d'Orsay. How good can eating be when it's provided by a company so gigantic? Does size matter? I place ten euros to win thirty that it will satisfy me.

Someone in the queue strikes me. Not actually, but I find I'm drawn to a young woman with crinkly straw-blonde hair cascading to her elbows. She looks as if she's leapt out of a 1960s European celluloid romance — *A Man and a Woman*, say. But there's no man that I can see. A waisted long black woollen overcoat hugs her slim frame. She turns up an astrakhan collar about her ears and dances lightly in the glacial temperature. She is booted to the knees in black suede. We exchange glances and she smiles. I'm not leaving the front of the queue. On the other hand, I wouldn't be averse to her joining me. She doesn't.

As icicles begin to droop from our noses and the children's crying intensifies, the great ticket computers of the Eiffel Tower boot up. The staff behind the glass go back to their labours — reluctantly, if I'm any judge of body language. We've waited thirty-five minutes. For 4.10 euros I buy admission to the first level. (It's 11 euros to the summit.) Nobody buys tickets just to the first or second levels, but the top of the tower is in cloud most of the time today and visibility is terrible even at ground level. (And, yes, I'm mean, as I've mentioned, and have been to the summit before.)

The lift is big enough to take scores of people. It fills quickly. One of the last small spaces is near me in the back corner. The girl in the black overcoat with the astrakhan collar sidles across, a microscopic grin on her lips. I take a stab:

'First time in Paris?'

'Yes,' she squeaks. Her voice is ludicrous. I try to hide my surprise. It's like the Métro's brakes between Invalides and La Tour Maubourg. It's so eccentric, I wonder if she's putting it on. Perhaps she has an awful disease. She's from Phoenix, Arizona, she says.

'And you?'

I fill her in. As the doors close, she tells me she's a critical-care nurse, and I say the usual stuff — nothing brilliant, unfortunately, but then I never shine in these situations. Just, like, wow, you must see appalling things. Heck. Gee! I don't know how you do it. She nods away politely, saying in a resigned, sad way that she's gotten used to the traumas. How long is she here, I ask. A week.

The lift scythes upwards through the tower's drab steel skeleton and level one arrives in no time. I'm the only one getting off, and I push through the others. 'Might see you on the way down,' I suggest pathetically, as the doors close. She smiles and waves.

Altitude 95 is a huge brasserie designed in retro-tech, *Dr Who* style. Beyond its walls of glass is the muscular superstructure of the tower itself. Inside, the colour scheme is battleship grey, the heads of large rivets border table tops, and convex mirrors bend all the harsh angles. Service trolleys are made from a burnished alloy that could plate a DC3 fuselage, and tub chairs have riveted steel backs. But it must have been done some time ago, because constant use has made everything seem just a little chipped and tired.

Very few lunchers are in, and I'm taken to bench seating well away from a table of six who smoke. Smoking in restaurants will soon be banned in France, says the maitre d'. He can't wait. The French have no respect for non-smokers, he adds.

Altitude 95's dishes cost less than half the price of those at the Jules Verne. Four entrées precede five main courses and seven desserts. You can eat skate wing with capers and lemon or seafood risotto with olive 'petals' for 22 euros, coq au vin for 23 euros and steak tartare with chips and salad for the same price. Desserts cost 8.80 euros.

What interest me most, however, are two menus: three courses 'of the day' for 27.70 euros; or two courses for 21.50 euros. If they're good, the latter option is pretty much a bargain — bearing in mind that you're eating in possibly the world's most famous structure and, on a clear day, you can see all the way to where my belongings are probably getting pinched in the shadow of Sacré-Coeur. The cheaper menu offers six oysters or a '*parmentier*' soup with bacon batons, fishcake with whipped butter or beef bourguignon, and camembert or floating island (whipped egg-white on a *crème anglaise*).

Dishes are a little slow coming out, but they're delightful. Nothing flash, just good honest traditional tucker. Half-a-dozen oysters are freshly opened, juicy, still attached to their half-shells and as good as can be got. They're big, steadied on ice, and arrive with half a lemon, slices of an excellent sourdough bread, a pot of fine unsalted butter and a shallot-and-red-wine-vinegar sauce. This vinegar-shallot concoction is always served with oysters in France. It's pure acid, a stupid and thoughtless accompaniment. Beef burgundy — a hearty red-wine stew — is classically tasty and comes with acceptable green and white gnocchi topped with a *salsa* (blended herbs and oil); cubes of red capsicum, dwarf tomatoes and mushrooms accompany.

From where I sit, I can see quite a bit of the tower's level-one promenade. Perhaps half-a-dozen people stroll about, none of them, unfortunately, the critical-care nurse with the squeaky delivery and astrakhan collar. But my stuff might at this instant be making its way into the back of a beat-up Citroën van. I'm a little anxious, and I really shouldn't dally.

A globe glows dimly in the concierge's apartment. A smiling, short, dark woman of strong build and Iberian presence comes to the door. She is so sorry, she repeats a thousand times after I introduce myself. (My gear has been brought inside safely.) She introduces her husband, a neat, trim *gentilhomme* in a polo shirt and V-neck pullover. They rarely leave the building but had a family emergency today. But, more importantly, she says, they didn't know I was coming. One of them would have stayed behind to greet me and hand over the keys. Nothing surer, she says. She is so sorry. I explain that I'd exchanged emails with the agency and the owner and I thought everyone was up to speed. She wasn't told, says Madame Fernandez.

In two trips I take my stuff up the spiral staircase, which curls tighter than a corkscrew. Its oak treads are a timber timpani in the stairwell, and I can imagine the music several people rushing up and down at once would make. There's a black-painted metal banister for free hands. The apartment is on the fourth floor, says Madame Fernandez, and I'll get used to the climb. (There is no lift.) Actually, it's very good for you, she offers. I know, I say, gasping.

Madame Galena's two-piece (as this type of accommodation is called) is spectacularly comfortable. It has a separate bedroom, small dining and sitting rooms joined by an arch, a good-sized bathroom, galley kitchen and corridor. It resonates with charm. It's a very Parisian apartment, but it's also a home. Someone cares about it. White walls seem freshly painted and are hung with muted prints and small abstract canvases. A sprinter making his way through a midnight sky the colour of van Gogh's starry night takes up one wall. Goya has influenced its creation. Rush mats cover most of the broad, grey-painted floorboards and ruched drapes in mid-grey organza hang in the tall windows. Like many thousands of Parisian apartments in old buildings, it has been renovated and modernised for warmth, charm and practicality. I'm not sure that the fireplace works, and I'm not game to light up. But its surround is in worked black marble. A mirror above it has a dazzling lime-green frame. Bookshelves are filled with serious reading across many fields, including philosophy and left-wing European politics. There's not a coffee-table tome in sight, and the small television set is there possibly only because the agency asked Madame Galena to install it. Its rabbit-ear aerial is pretty useless.

At around five o'clock the phone in the apartment rings. It's Madame Galena herself, calling from Italy. She is so apologetic. And between pardons, she delivers stinging serves about the agency. *She* didn't know I was arriving today, she avers. But, I say, I received an email in excellent English saying that all was well. And I replied to it. Ah, she says, that can't be right. Her English is very poor, she says. Perhaps they wrote the email for her, she offers. All is well, I say, and no harm has been done. I'm happy and the apartment is wonderful, I tell her. And she hangs up after wishing me the very best possible stay in Paris.

So, at times like these it appears to be the same wherever you are in the world. The buck is volleyed from person to person, and to discover the truth of an incident might occupy the term of an examining magistrate's natural life. Frankly, I couldn't care less. Nothing has been stolen, and I'm in the apartment. What's more, I'm going to enjoy being here, even if it is without the full-sized bath that starred in Monsieur Montebello's.

I'm anticipating a wallow in a glorious bog of nostalgia at Vaudeville, which we always called 'the' Vaudeville in the 1970s. (Michelin, actually, drops the definite article; Group Flo, which owns it, calls it *Le* Vaudeville.) I'm dining there tonight for old time's sake. But also in memory of Rolly Pullen, my favourite journalist.

For many years from the 1950s, Rolly was Paris correspondent for Melbourne's *Herald & Weekly Times*. He also strung for the Beaverbrook papers in London. He died quite a while ago, but to know him in the 1970s was never to forget him. He held court in the

Vaudeville, decades-younger anglophone journalists from Agence France-Presse worshipping at his feet, as it were. I was one of them.

I descend into the light-sparkled blackness of the boulevard de Rochechouart and head towards the Métro. Fifty metres along the road, a stationary car is on fire near the corner of the rue de Clignancourt. It's in the oncoming slow lane. A ball of flame burns sulphurously, licking out from its engine bay and around the bonnet. A few onlookers — including young French Africans — watch from a distance, some of them mightily amused. There is nobody within thirty metres of the car, and I notice a sole police officer on the wide median strip, keeping back a few spectators. Within a minute, flames have grown to engulf the front half of the car. Small explosions and muted *phuts* burst from the inferno. Flames drip onto the bitumen and set it alight.

I'm one of only two people taking photographs, and I wonder if I should try to break through the *flic's* imaginary perimeter to get a better picture. I'm getting OK shots, but they're from too far away. They're images the whole world knows, anyway — clichés after the events of recent weeks. The blackness. Fireball in the night. Reflected light off the door pillars and shattered windows of the car that's been torched. I'm reminded of a classic on the cover of *The Economist* in recent weeks, a real top Press shot: legs braced wide apart, a fireman arcs a hose over his back. His right hand holds the nozzle, directing it at the flames leaping from the rear of a hatchback.

Amid a cacophony of klaxoning, *pompiers* (firemen) and more police arrive. I snap away. By now the car is completely engulfed. Flames light up the rollerdoors of the shops on the footpath. They leap three metres into the night. The car explodes noisily, small pieces of shrapnel shooting several metres in all directions. Three firemen roll out a slim hose in seconds. One grabs the nozzle and gives me the snap I want. He's between me and the car, the reflective strips on his black suit a dazzling silver, his metal helmet brilliant. He arcs the hose around his waist, points the nozzle and lets fly. The jet is fine and wide — just like you'd use on a flower bed — and in a dervish of energy, he crushes the flames. In twenty seconds, a mushroom cloud of steam the size of a hot-air balloon rises above the boulevard, filtering the night. So close to home, I think, but it's happening everywhere. And for reasons the perpetrators believe to be sound.

---

As Fats Waller said, the joint is jumping. Vaudeville is hugely popular — full, in fact. I've eaten here a couple of times in recent years, but in the 1970s, when it was independently owned and prices were lower, it was something of a canteen for the journalists of Agence France-Presse, the French newsagency. AFP's headquarters were handily placed on an adjacent side of the place de la Bourse.

I recall exquisite cold salmon with a superb house-made mayonnaise costing about 11 francs. You won't get a glass of water in today's Vaudeville for 11 francs (say, 2 euros). Some years ago, Groupe Flo bought it. Paris's dominant restaurant group is named after the capital's famous Brasserie Flo and counts 160 restaurants (some are franchises) in several countries in its stable. In the firm's Flo Brasseries division alone there are 23 restaurants, including the well-known Bofinger, Julien, Terminus nord and La Coupole, where I shall dine tomorrow night. And let's just say that the incorporation of brasseries results in variable experiences. Economies of scale are no doubt made, and I suspect that some food preparation is done in central commissary kitchens. Nonetheless, in recent years I've eaten a couple of quite acceptable meals at Vaudeville.

Groupe Flo also owns the Hippopotamus chain of steak restaurants. But rapid expansion from its base, which began with eating places but soon included high-class catering, has caused big financial problems — what one commentator understatedly described as a 'delicate financial situation'. In short, the group has a huge debt, but Jean-Paul Bucher, the big man who founded the firm, is apparently sanguine. He believes in diversity.

Vaudeville is an exquisite art-deco construction. Most of its interior is faced with veined stone in a shimmering honeycomb colour. Huge vases hold enormous bouquets of the brightest flowers, and there are mirrors, bevelled edges and elegant etchings. Thin black-lacquered steel columns support the lot.

I'm shown to a bench seat against a wall — always more to see looking out — between a Benelux family and three young male American executives (Americans sustain many of Paris's restaurants). To my left, the couple is in early middle age, their son and daughter teenagers. They're all big-boned people with dark tans and jolly demeanours. They volley comments across the table in an explosive gutteral language and laugh a lot. Flemish, I guess. Nearest me is the girl, who has bright yellow hair coiffed into a glittering bob. Her eyes are sapphires. Despite the frigid air outside, her tight little top and pubic-low jeans expose a vast expanse of flesh the colour of dark chocolate. A tattoo of a broadsword points down over her coccyx and disappears between her cheeks. She is so tanned the blade is black — I can't imagine it was originally that colour. Her skin is uniformly smooth, the grain so fine that I want to touch it. But I also don't want a *panier à salade* (divisional van) to take me away.

The American blokes are just plain boring. Indeed, what they say is like killer radiation — so exclusive and from such a different world that inoculations might be advised before going near them. They're carriers of PV: pretentious virus. Next week one *has* to go to New York. The week after the second *must* be in Washington. The third can't make a date any time this month or next, he says. He's in Frankfurt, London, Beijing, then LA. He's trying to avoid a Sydney trip, he sniffs. His mates are trumped.

Vaudeville's list is an inventory of standard fare. No surprises here. You'll find something you like, though — bound to — among hot and cold starters, five specialities, fish and meat dishes, and grills. Wild-pig terrine with a red-wine jelly, fresh and smoked salmon rillettes, six burgundy snails (in garlic butter) and onion soup cost from 7 to 10 euros. Among five specials are a beef *entrecôte* with bearnaise or bordelaise sauce for 28 euros and *tête de veau* for 17.50 euros.

My Scottish salmon *à la graine de moutarde* (16.90 euros) sounds grand, but it's actually disappointing. A chunk of fish is cut in half like a sandwich, its filling grain mustard and a couple of sprigs of tarragon. Another sprig sits on top, and a lacklustre brown sauce pools on the plate. Small cubes of tomato punctuate the sauce. It would be unusual to be served underdone fish in France, and my salmon is cooked through and on the point of fraying. Included in the order is a small dish of baby leeks *au gratin* — browned off in the oven. Their sauce is watery. A tiramisu (7.50 euros) is equally unexciting. Arriving in a glass tumbler, it lacks creaminess, alcohol and coffee, the bases of a good tiramisu.

As one of the guys next to me abjures 'half-assed business plans' and the girl with the dark-chocolate tan flirts with a waiter in English, my eyes inevitably settle on Rolly's table at the back of the room. People are sitting at it, of course, which affronts me more than somewhat, as another knockabout journalist of considerable talent, Damon Runyon, would have said. They have no idea what it means. Its history.

The years rewind, and I see Rolly trudging between Vaudeville's tables, grim as usual. Across the mosaic floor tiles in yellow and black and blue he arrives at that table. He greets the AFP boys, removes his stylish grey fedora and plain maroon scarf, unbuttons his gabardine raincoat and astonishes us with the happenings of the day. (He used to file his copy from the telegraph office beside the agency.)

Rolly was not a handsome man — his eyes were the size of nailheads, his hooked nose was small and his face shone — but his physiognomy took on rapt animation when he told a story. And his stories were always fabulous but true. He was the first reporter to reveal that the Duke of Windsor was dangerously ill: Rolly was himself in the American Hospital getting a skin lesion removed in 1972 when he saw Edward shuffling along its corridors. A couple of days later Rolly was out and telling us that he'd just filed a piece saying the former King of England appeared to be near death.

Brigitte Bardot asked him to jump into bed with her after an interview in the south of France. (I don't think that that was unusual at Brigitte's house, by the way.) But as I understood his complex psyche, Rolly had largely given away women following a tragic love affair. In grief, he had sought reclusion in Paris in the early 1950s to become a professional organist. (Another reason why he appealed to me so much; I wanted to be a pianist.) There were great instruments in so many of the city's churches, he used to say. He was obsessed with listening to them, and some he had played. But he had never been a professional musician, becoming, somehow or other, a superlative reporter instead.

He got a scoop when Nobel prizewinner Albert Schweitzer made a rare excursion to the world beyond his mission hospital at Lambaréné in equatorial Gabon. Rolly, of course, knew all about Schweitzer's Bach scholarship. His story went that he had heard part of the great man's journey out of Africa was to be by train. He got into Schweitzer's carriage at some remote location, found the doctor's compartment and sat opposite him. Then he began practising the pedal part — the line of music you play with your feet — of a well-known Bach fugue. Schweitzer was all eyes. Rolly told the old man not to mind him, leant over confidentially and said he was practising a piece of music for organ. You know, with the pipes, he said, gesturing. Churches? Concert coming up. Scweitzer smiled and told him who he was. The great Albert Schweitzer — doctor, theologian, missionary and musicologist. And he wagged a finger at Rolly and told him the name of the piece he was pretending to play. Rolly feigned astonishment. They talked for hours. Rolly got his scoop.

But the Rolly story that made the most impact on me concerned the terrible Mercedes crash at Le Mans in 1955. Rolly had been sent to cover the famous 24-hour race by Express newspapers. But motoring editor Robert Glenton, whom I recall as a fairly stout and ebullient man by the time I was briefly his colleague in 1970, wanted Rolly in particular to monitor the Jaguar team's performance. The English firm had only got back into motor sport the previous year with its D-type, which was designed to win at Le Mans.

Rolly had no interest in motor cars, let alone racing them. In no time the Press tent bored him and he wandered off among the spectators lining the main straight, more lonely than a crowd. He walked right into the world's worst motor-racing accident, witnessing it at close range. A Mercedes hit an embankment and cartwheeled into spectators. Magnesium in its body burned white-hot. The engine, bonnet and front axle scythed through men, women and children. (Eighty-two were killed and seventy-six injured.) Uninjured himself, Rolly took in the carnage, and began running... away from the Press tent (his instincts for an exclusive story were always perfect).

The very long Le Mans circuit in those days passed through several small villages. Rolly ran for a kilometre or so until he found a village and a phone. He got through to Robert Glenton. The *Sunday Express's* Saturday afternoon deadline was fast approaching — as I recall it was about 6 pm — and Rolly gabbled the news. He had seen the fireball and the cartwheeling Mercedes. Bodies everywhere. Carnage. War zone. Absolutely awful. Dozens killed. He could file, he told Robert, a front-page lead off the top of his head, as the saying goes.

'That's all well and good, old boy,' said Robert, according to Rolly, 'but how are Jaguar doing?'

# day nine

I'm off to the Louvre to see what's on the menu. There'll be a range of eating outlets, from posh to simple, I'm sure. Something for everyone, and I hope that what I eventually consume will be as satisfying as lunch at the Eiffel Tower. The same company will be providing it.

When I first came to Paris, as you might remember, I thought the French capital smelt of upmarket biscuits. Perhaps I was a little overawed at the time. I can see what I meant (and it still has a strong compelling sweetness) but, as I negotiate the streets and passageways nowadays, I wonder if there's an inordinate contribution of waste to Paris's perfume. Two sorts come to mind: beyond the tourist precincts, Parisian footpaths remain dog lavatories. Several determined bids have been mounted over many years to solve the problem. I seem to recall specialist vacuumers on motor scooters, and, lately, three-wheeled machines that were supposed to do the job. Stiff fines apply to owners who don't clean up after their hounds, but it doesn't seem to make much difference. Just the other day near the grandiose entrance of the Banque de France I squashed a pile of dog excrement the size of an elephant's dropping. In short, keep your head down around town. Get your bearings, then drop your gaze.

And the other overwhelming waste smell in Paris is stale urine. You notice it in corridors and sometimes in the streets, in lanes, alleys and doorways. Much of it is contributed by *clochards* — tramps — who live out here amid the traffic and pedestrians. They are *clochards*, by the way, because at the old Les Halles markets in the centre of the city a bell (*une cloche*) was rung early in the mornings to give away perishable food. The *clochards* came running.

The Louvre and its surrounds are suitably sanitised. Dog doodles are distanced. I take the down escalators beneath the glass pyramid in this huge palace's forecourt. Down is the way in, even if you have to ascend to first and second levels to see the gallery's best-known works. Shaped like an enormous U, the Louvre has thousands of works on display and many more thousands vaulted. I often think a person of wide average interests could spend at least a week investigating it, just to get an idea of its scope, the breadth of the collection. A specialist could equally spend a week, say, studying Etruscan antiquities, the art of Pharaonic Egypt, or nineteenth century French painters.

The whole of the second floor is closed today — it's winter almost — which means I won't be able to glance at a couple of my favourites: Watteau's *Pierrot* and Ingres's wonderful *Turkish Bath*. But that leaves untold numbers of other statues, canvases, inscriptions, bronzes, pieces of jewellery, silverware, ceramics, icons, furniture and so on. I love the vastness of Géricault's *Raft of the Medusa*. And in David's painting of Napoleon's coronation, palace intrigue is cunningly revealed through the inadequately disguised expressions on several faces. I always find the people looking at the *Mona Lisa* more interesting than the painting itself. I wish I understood why, they're saying, this is supposed to be so good. How did it inspire that mega-seller? (Actually, they're not putting it like that, but they should be.) Today, a group of Koreans puzzle over da Vinci's deftness. An Italian couple — bluster in metres of well-cut waterproofing — congratulate themselves on their nationality.

But I'm here to see what there is to eat, and the time it takes to track down the various cafés and restaurants surprises me. Le Grand Louvre on the entrance level is officially described as a 'gastronomical restaurant'. Through the glass, it certainly looks the part, tables set luxuriously. You'll eat six oysters here for 14 euros, a crayfish salad with lentil and eel aspic for 12 euros, and a duck foie gras terrine (cold slices) for 18 euros. A fillet of bass on a bisque sauce with rice is 28 euros, leg of lamb with haricot-bean purée costs 26 euros, and roasted saddle of rabbit with a morel sauce is 29 euros. A fixed menu with some choice costs 29 euros for two courses, 37 euros for three. Three cafés distributed widely through the Louvre offer far less interesting fare — a toasted ham-and-cheese sandwich for 8 euros and a plate of club sandwiches for 13 euros, for instance.

Frankly, I'm about to go home in despair when I notice the fairly constant stream of gallery-goers heading for La Cafétéria de la Pyramide on the mezzanine level. I discover a gem. Choice is comprehensive, beginning with a plate of *charcuterie* comprising three thin slices of a large-diameter salami, four much thicker ones of a smaller sausage, a slice of country terrine and a slice of paté in a crust with a thick layer of jelly on top. Gherkins, salad, two small tomatoes and a bread roll share this generous dish. And it's for sale at 6.95 euros, or 8 euros with nearly two (Australian standard) glasses of new beaujolais. You can compose your own salad and pay between 3.30 euros and 8 euros depending on the size of the bowl you put it in. There are tabouli and corn, olives and hard-boiled eggs, big cubes of cold parsleyed pork, hosts of salad greens of several sorts, tomatoes, radishes, cucumber, broccoli and, no doubt, several other things that I fail to note. You can buy portions of fresh apple tart, raspberry torte and strawberry flan. And there are individual lemon meringue pies with swirly browned-off tops. Blocks of rich chocolate slices are stamped with gold leaf. Hot main dishes served from *bains marie* are a steal: lasagne costs 7.70 euros, braised ham 8.70 and salmon 9 euros.

I order *travers* (spare ribs) of pork baked with honey (9 euros), help myself to a half-bottle of wine and a bread roll, and head for the cashier. When I ask the smiling African Frenchman behind the till how I get my wine opened, he hands me a waiter's friend. He asks if I know how to use it. 'You've got nothing to worry about,' I tell him.

I find a place in the scrupulously clean and well-lighted eating space. There are plenty of empty white plywood chairs at lots of cleared white laminated table tops. My ribs, a succulent tanned block the size of a robust pencil case, are excellent. They're sweet and salty, tasty and chewy. Green peppercorns are strewn on top, genuine cooking juices are flavoursome, and the garnishes are an excellent potato purée and a vegetable stew containing carrot discs, beans of two sorts and eggplant cubes. My little *beaujolais nouveau* — Eugene Brocard — is fine. It costs 4.40 euros. So, a very hearty lunch for 14 euros. Paper napkins on demand, and help yourself to pitchers of water and ice.

---

Paul Bocuse, the doyen of French chefs, told me ten or so years ago that even his most eminent colleagues were waking up. They could see the writing on the wall. People didn't want to — couldn't — any longer pay vast amounts to eat super-refined dishes served by battalions of waiters in regal surroundings. It was why even he had opened cheaper bistros. Eating out needed to be simpler and more casual to suit the *Zeitgeist* (although that wasn't a word *le grand Paul* would use).

So I need to check what's being served at a couple of places opened recently by veteran star chefs. Joël Robuchon, for instance, was the most talked about cook of the 1980s. His mashed potato was legendary. Then he got out of the game altogether to write a newspaper column. Recently, though, he has returned to restaurants with two Parisian outlets — a '*table*' and an '*atelier*' (workshop) — that are considerably cheaper than his three-Michelin-starred restaurant of the 1980s, Jamin, where you could eat a cold caviar jelly surfaced thinly with cauliflower cream, individual fish eggs dotting its edge in a perfect annulus.

I cross the river and make my way down the rue du Bac to the elegant rue de Montalembert in the seventh arrondissement. Robuchon's L'Atelier is a cave of a place where no bookings are taken for lunch. (You can make dinner reservations, but only for 6.30 pm.) Low-ceilinged, it feels cramped and funky, two dining spaces — some at a type of bar — on either side of a central kitchen. Stylish and wealthy Parisians, most of them well into middle-age, sit on stools and chairs while young — and even younger — cooks learn their craft in the kitchen, searing, whipping and blending ingredients, sometimes enthusiastically and at other moments listlessly. I can't see anyone who might appear to have significant experience, let alone Monsieur Robuchon himself.

I decide not to eat after I scan the lists of dishes handed over by a sniffy manager. Twenty-one small servings are labelled '*dégustation*', meaning 'tasting size', and you should order several of them to make a meal. Then follow ten entrées and nine fish and meat dishes. Prices vary widely: among the small portions are a gazpacho with croutons for 10 euros and a butterflied fillet of beef with 'pastoral' savours for 26 euros. You can get an egg with fungal cream for 16 euros or marinated anchovies with an eggplant '*confite*' for 11 euros. An entrée of vitello tonnato will set you back 21 euros and a rabbit terrine 19 euros. Prices lift considerably with mains, where thyme-flavoured milk-fed lamb costs 36 euros, suckling pig on a spit the same, and veal's liver with onion rings and a sour sauce is priced at 39 euros.

No dishes really excite me. Many are pale imitations of New World originality, remaining cautious and tentative.

I suspect that some of the tastes are very refined and balanced, but I'm used to heroic flavours these days — the heightened amplification cooks need to work into their offerings when bold foodstuffs such as chilli and lemongrass, coriander and lime, say, are employed. I don't want to have to search for subtlety any more. I no longer need or want super-*saveur*-sophistication in a bistro (not that there's any guarantee the *atelier* will dish it up). Reviews have been variable: one by Gastroville scoring it twelve out of twenty and complaining about less-than-the-best makings. It implied that some were stale. A single scallop cost 18 euros and a single crustacean ravioli, 25 euros. 'Are we on the verge of seeing gourmet McDonald's?' it asked.

I retrace my steps, take the rue de Rivoli, then turn right into the rue Royale and walk up to the place de la Madeleine. This is where the chef's chef, Alain Senderens, opines from a certain gastro-intellectual *hauteur*. He's been critical in recent years of unadventurous French cooking. The rest of the world — especially the New one — has been streaking ahead, while Gallic cooks approach new tastes with timidity. And his response to the new challenge of more casual dining has been to convert his three-Michelin-starred restaurant into a new brasserie. It happened only weeks ago. More or less overnight, Lucas Carton, the veteran posh classic where a meal with house wine cost between 144 and 380 euros (and without wine between 138 and 229 euros), became simply Senderens. I used to look through the window here, having never eaten at Lucas Carton. Some of the luxurious furnishings seem to be gone, but Senderens remains a very stylish eating space.

These days the boss has a penchant for choosing food that goes with certain wines — not the other way around — and his new list recommends a glass, costing between 6 and 16 euros, for each dish. Entrées are priced between 18 and 30 euros, the latter a lobster and mango-basil salad, which is old hat where I come from. The cheapest starter is ricotta ravioli with lemonthyme and a whipped sage butter — equally fading fedora. French chefs still trust curry, a flavour they know and love, and Senderens' lamb chops come with a 'Javanese' curry that includes lemongrass and mango. It costs 39 euros. A fish and mussel curry costs 32 euros. I've tasted them all before, and both flavours and servings would, I suspect, be bigger where I come from.

I ate steak tartare for the first time at La Coupole, the quintessential Parisian brasserie. Steak tartare, you will remember, is raw minced beef blended with condiments such as a raw egg and finely chopped shallots, capers and parsley. 'Huns and Mongols', as an old French book of mine puts it, originated the recipe after tenderising beef under their saddles. Eaten at the temperature of a sweaty stallion, I suppose, it was reckoned to be a terrific winter pick-me-up.

By the time I went there in the early 1970s, La Coupole had for decades commanded custom from Left Bank writers and artists — as well as the upper bourgeoisie of the fourteenth arrondissement to the south. I dined there with my new wife Dominique, Pierre, my paella partner, and his wife Mireille, my sister-in-law. We were young — out for a night and a laugh. And La Coupole provided both those things. Its service was brusque and fast, the waiters' attitudes as highly strung as their bowties (their aprons were spotless). La Coupole was an attraction for genuine Parisians, the people who lived in the city, as well as its well-known clientele of artists, singers, writers and models. Since opening its doors in 1927 it had always been the case. The scandalous black *danseuse* Josephine Baker, photographer Man Ray, Picasso and Hemingway were regulars. And one of its most famous offerings was steak tartare.

I have only dim recollections of that first night at La Coupole, but the spectacular tessellated floor, the clatter of bistro chairs and the tartare itself are among them. (I can't recall having seen any celebrities.) In those days, a waiter brought the minced beef — all maroon and devoid of even the slightest skerrick of fat — for your perusal and approval. A beret of ground beast, it was topped by half an eggshell containing a raw yolk. The waiter would also bring small bowls of the traditional condiments — chopped capers, gherkins, parsley and onions. Under your direction, he would customise your tartare, giving you two or three tastings during the mixing process to confirm its rightness for your palate. (I have a suspicion oil and perhaps Worcestershire sauce were also offered.)

Groupe Flo bought La Coupole in 1988, and restored it immediately to its flapper-age glory. It's hard to overstate the importance of Parisian brasseries in the gastronomic scheme of things. They sit several affordable rungs below the great starred restaurants. Most visitors to Paris take their Gallic culinary bearings from them. Indeed, for the locals, too, they are mostly what dining out is all about. They are usually very big, crowded, businesslike, and make their very own special kind of music: a symphony scored for excited voices, cutlery on plates and the periodic popping of champagne corks. And they offer the same canonic dishes, year in and year out, cooked in the same ways. Their gastronomic contribution has far-distant origins: Alsatian refugees from the 1870 Franco-Prussian war set up the first Parisian brasseries. A 'brasserie', after all, is a brewery, and the model for the Parisian brasserie is the German *bierkeller*. (Families from Auvergne in central France also owned many of the capital's brasseries.)

From the boulevard du Montparnasse you can see beyond the glass-fronted café into the enormous square room that is La Coupole itself. By 8 pm about a dozen people are waiting for tables, but I'm shown straight in because I'm alone. And I immediately remember the mosaic floor and its modernistic chevrons and half-rings in cream and off-white, brown and black, even the way the brown leather banquettes, tables and oak dining chairs with their studded leather backs are set up in an enormous grid. In the centre of the room is something of a golden dome (but hardly a spectacular *coupole*), a sleek abstract statue of a pair of dancers under it. I ask for a non-smoking table. The waiter leads me to a far corner of this immense space, taking rights and lefts through the grid. La Coupole seats hundreds and is said to be Paris's biggest dining room.

Waistcoated waiters, and the sheer numbers of staff and diners, suggest I'm in for a *correct* eating experience, as the French say, even if it's probably not going to send me into raptures. I take a seat on a banquette facing a wall three or so metres away. Behind me, a little above a partition of honeyed wood, two thick brass rails run parallel to hold hats and gloves, overcoats and bags. The room is splendid. Lustrous oaks empanels much of it, of course, but there are also mirrors and murals of showgirls and nymphs. Two dozen square, moss-green columns with gilt capitals are an especially revered feature. Almost three dozen artists — several of them of considerable renown — are said to have painted the original images, which Groupe Flo restored.

In the great brasseries you should stick to the simple offerings for which they are famous. *Choucroute garni* is the best-known — nothing more nor less than sauerkraut topped with pork of various sorts, usually sausages and belly straps. La Coupole serves seafood platters at a range of prices; lots of half-dozen oysters priced between 13.20 and 19.50 euros, depending on size, origin and species; house-made pigs' trotters (12.50 euros); fresh tagliatelle (17.50 euros); and steak of several sorts.

My napkin is enormous, white and worked, and the tablecloths are equally rich. You use dazzling alloy cutlery, and if you look carefully you'll notice that the logo on the plates features a naked young lady with a 1920s bob sitting between an artist's palate and an open book. It's a lovely — very Gallic

— image; the young woman is torn between decadence and the thrill of thinking. So many famous Frenchwomen, Colette in the vanguard, have been thus. La Coupole is used to flirting with decadence. On the walls hang black-and-white photographs, taken between the wars, of crowd scenes inside the dining room. Look at the smiles on the faces! It was an era when libertine attitudes were more or less mandatory — as was seeing a priest to confess the following day.

I muse on what life must have been like for Felix Del Prado, billed as the '*chanteur*' with La Coupole's celebrated Bachichia orchestra. He peers into the distance opposite me, looking disconsolate. A dark brilliantined bow-wave of hair sits above his forehead, and a white scarf is knotted around his neck. His billowing satin shirt shines. Perhaps it was pink. With a ten-gallon hat he could be crooning in Nevada, a singing cowboy.

Three fillets of Baltic herring (7 euros) are said to be served with fresh cream. Soused in oil, they are good, but the cream component is really only a watery white sauce containing a couple of discs of carrot and cubes of apple. A sprig of thyme and a bay leaf garnish. And, although I'm in a non-smoking section, the sweet, obnoxious smell of burning tobacco reaches me as I swallow my last mouthful of fish. A chap has lit up not two metres away. I alert a senior waiter. Is he allowed to smoke? *Oui monsieur*, he may, says the waiter. But this is a non-smoking section, I say. I asked to be brought to a non-smoking part of the restaurant. Yes, says the waiter, who is quickly tiring of me, he may smoke there, where he is smoking, but not here, where you are. Those tables are for smokers. You are unfortunately near them. Pure logic. Come in René Descartes. Where the smoker is sitting, and where I am sitting, is beyond doubt. It's also beyond doubt that they are only a metre or two apart. But I'm not going to win any war I wage on this one: La Coupole is full, and I'm halfway through dinner.

I'm quite excited to be eating steak tartare here again after so many years. I expect to enjoy the mixing ritual. But I notice a couple of waiters at their station a few metres away. Their backs are turned and they're whipping away. Within seconds my tartare is in front of me — ready-mixed. No tastings, no exhibition of components, no trial runs. There's your steak tartare, *monsieur*, now eat it. Which I do, and it isn't bad at all. But I prefer the way La Coupole used to do things. And I should add that my meal's highlight is sublime chips. One of the first things you notice about eating in France is the tastiness of French potatoes, no matter their size or variety. They are *formidable*, and La Coupole's chips have a sweetness and strength of flavour that are astonishing. Moreover, they have been cooked properly. Super-crisp on the outside, their insides amount to stratospherically tasty, blow-away spud-froth.

I'll take a promenade for a while, but return later for La Coupole's 'salsa' night in the basement. Should be fun. Pleasure remains pre-eminent in Paris, and careful observation reinforces clichés. Portly and of no great physical presence, either of them, two white-haired chaps sit metres apart in La Coupole's glassed-in café. Each has a gorgeous girl opposite him, who, in years, might tally a third of his age. They cuddle the girls, one of them fondling an exposed thigh. At La Coupole, especially, it's meant to happen. While staring at one — all right, perhaps in envy (of his money, of course) — I'm almost tripped up by a feisty terrier. Little more than a bundle of butterscotch-coloured fluff darting erratically on nude legs a few centimetres above the footpath, the pooch has been given too long a leash. Its owner is a *grande dame* of wide thoroughfares out for an evening constitutional. Her hair is 'done' so that no strand should displace by more than a millimetre during the week between visits to the *coiffeuse*, and her lipsticked mouth is as red as a stop light. She purses it. 'Adolf, you little villain,' she tells the dog.

I'm back for early entry to the salsa, paying 16 euros admission and another few to check in my leather bomber jacket, gloves, hat and backpack. Leaving them in the *vestiaire* is obligatory. You enter the *dansant* with only dignity, your lightly clad self and a wallet. I'm given two chits. One is for a free drink at the bar, the other to recover my belongings. Already animated, the basement is the size of a country hall. Ninety-five per cent of its area is dance-floor. I get a (cheap, as it happens) beer at a long, damp timber bar. There is no 'live' band. Latin brass bleats through amplifiers and loudspeakers somewhere, or perhaps everywhere, in the room. And the dancers, especially the girls, look terrifically expert. They fill the floor. Their sways and swivels are precise, sensuous and complex. They match the titillations of the beat, and it's all done at frenetic pace.

It occurs to me that someone has taught all these people how to discipline their bodies in such a way; how to *do* this stuff. Of course! Preceding La Coupole's salsa nights is a one-hour course (22.50 euros). They must have all attended it at some stage, I reason. Women are accepting invitations to dance from anyone who asks — African French, north African French and even pug-ugly white mugs. It seems to be the etiquette. Or perhaps they just know their faces from the salsa classes. And there seems to be a ritual associated with taking your partner onto the dance-floor. Men are leading their ladies with a kind of archaic gallantry, their hands held high. They must be taught that, too. It almost looks as if they're from the eighteenth century — about to trip off a little *minuet* or *quadrille*.

But the salsa is another dance altogether. My mother and other Methodists would have fainted had they seen three seconds of it. Some couples are grinding away in such perfect time, their bodies for all intents and purposes welded together. Their simultaneous and shimmering elevations and descents, twists, bends and sways, are intended to arouse. Them — but also we who watch. The voyeur in me conquers, and for a second or two I feel like yelling at one bloke, all hips and thrusts, 'Aaaawwww, why don't you just fuck her and be done with it!' (But I'd like to keep the *panier à salade* well away from La Coupole tonight.) I don't dance, of course, not knowing how to. I'm envious, angry and ashamed all at once. It reminds me too painfully of the youth I never had, the Bible that stole my being.

Then I realise I've lost the stub to get my clothes back. (And my camera — new — is in my jacket.) I panic. I check all my pockets. I check them again. And a third time. It has gone all right, but it's somewhere in this room, by now probably ground to dust under Cuban heels, jogging shoes and stilettos, or saturated with beer and glued to the sticky top of one of the basement's few low tables. I've got to leave immediately. I've got to try to explain my predicament to the *vestiaire* girl.

She's sympathetic, but the incoming queue is about twenty-strong. She has to deal with them first. *Then* she will look for me. Five minutes pass, and the queue for the salsa night just gets longer. I appeal to her. It won't take a second, I suggest. She asks me what time I entered — it's crucial. Behind her are racks, metres upon metres, of swaddlings of every description. Can I see how difficult the task is going to be? She returns to the incoming queue, taking mountains of fake furs, anoraks and *vestes* in her arms. I wait ten minutes before she turns away from those arriving. Describe the jacket again, she demands — in detail. I do. She disappears to the back of the cloakroom. I see movement. An elephant appears to have got into the back of an aid truck distributing garments. Seconds later, she re-appears with my *blouson*. And scarf and gloves. The camera is in the pocket. I am effusive with thanks — can't thank her enough. She smiles and returns to the arrivals. I mount the stairs alone against their tide (I'll bet all of them can dance). Out in the boulevard, it's arctic and the zip of my jacket has broken. I'll have to clutch it around me for the rest of my stay.

# day ten

It's ironic that an exhibition on the achievements of Arabs in science and technology coincides with the blazing cars. I'm about to marvel at the gigantic contribution they have made to mathematics (think algebra and algorithm, for instance), geography, medicine, chemistry, and more mundane but useful pursuits such as irrigation. In the Métro to the Institut du Monde Arabe, I give up my place to an elderly gentleman whose wife has taken the jumpseat alongside me. Smiling, he thanks me, telling me I am *'très aimable'* — a gentleman, in other words. (It's just an expression, and doesn't really mean 'very loveable'.) Their dress is careful and correct, his tweed sports jacket fitting perfectly. Métro trains accelerate quickly and as we pull out of the Cité station I lose my balance for an instant. The old chap grabs and steadies me. I thank him. The couple and I change trains at Odéon and, as we get out, he and his wife say goodbye to me.

The institute was an item in President François Mitterand's programme of great architectural works built between 1981 and 1995. A joint venture of France and several Arab nations, it houses a museum, library and auditorium. But it's most well known for its eight-hundred-square-metre south-facing wall. From the broad plaza at its base, the wall is like a chessboard of Turkish tiles. But, rather than the usual blue and white, each tile is composed of shining metallic rings and rectangles. Thirty thousand light-sensitive irises open and close according to the amount of sun striking them. Their purpose is to control the heat and illumination inside the institute, but the building as a whole is the kind of extravagant architectural gesture that's characteristic of Parisian history — the Eiffel Tower being the best known. Moreover, critics say the institute's wall has never really worked properly.

I walk straight into the exhibition — no queues — and I wish Paris's European French and African French and North African French and Levantine French would come here in droves to see the display. It's sparse, but stylish and orderly, exposing an immense treasury of Arab intellect. There are ancient astronomical charts, engraved brass devices that determine the positions of heavenly bodies, life-sized diagrams showing blood circulation, audiovisuals explaining ingenious irrigation systems and war machines, sound grabs of Arabian music accompanying explanations of its complexities, and pages and pages under glass of early Arabian discoveries in mathematics that built on Greek and Indian work.

The Arabian contribution to human culture is simply overwhelming, yet most of us are ignorant of it. I wish the *flics* who stop the boys in the Métro would come here, look and think. Look up, too. How many of us realise that, while many names of heavenly bodies have Greek and Latin origins, many hundreds of others were either renamed or discovered by Arabs? (Al Dab'aran, A'crab, Al Zirr and Sched'ar have a singular poetry.) Look up, look up, this exhibition demands of us. I am moved by a video clip of a white-haired European-French intellectual who frames in a matter of minutes the contribution of Arab minds to humanity. It's remiss of me not to note his name, but I feel now that it looked Jewish.

I ask myself many questions as I sit down for a late lunch at the ground-floor Café Litteraire. Why can't humans be less prejudiced? Why aren't we more reasonable? Why are we so unkind to others? Why are we naturally racist? In short, why are humans human? I'm reminded of something you hear constantly about particularly bad human behavior. Someone — often a chorus — will scream, 'What an animal! This hoon acted like animal! He committed an animal act!' 'No, he didn't,' I'm always tempted to reply. 'It was the act of a human... Other animals don't behave so badly.'

My table is of marble, my deep vinyl bench-seat is comfortable and floor-to-ceiling glass gives onto the plaza. Institute employees take a smoking break. At a distant table, an elderly French couple play hide-and-seek with their toddling granddaughter. Beyond the plaza you might expect to see several Arab-leaning restaurants. But all I see is one of Groupe Flo's answers to fast food — prompt porterhouse in the shape of a Buffalo Grill.

A laminated list of a dozen or so dishes in the Litteraire has colour photographs of such offerings as the *assiette dégustation*, which features eight Lebanese titbits (four cold, four hot) including tabouli, hummus and smoked eggplant (12.50 euros). Dips and salad with slices of marinated meats costs the same.

A waiter tells me that, because it's late, only the couscous is available. There was a terrific run on other items at midday, apparently. Everything but the couscous is sold out. It's a couscous '*maison*', though, which is priced at 12 euros. I take it, and order a half-bottle of Clos St Thomas, a Lebanese rosé from the Békaa Valley. (The Lebanese would probably argue about that spelling, putting a 'q' where the 'k' is. I'm of the T. E. Lawrence — of Arabia — school of thought: in the same manuscript he often spelt proper names in several different ways. There is no 'right' way when transliterating from a language that uses different symbols.)

Fairly quickly a huge plateful of food is put in front of me. There's the hindquarter of an enormous chook, big cylinders of carrot and chunks of celery, turnip pieces, swatches of cabbage, a few chickpeas and a dune of couscous. And it's all rather tasty, the chicken tender and juicy, but only lukewarm. I ask for chilli (which they don't understand in France — in an Arab restaurant you must ask for 'harissa') and salt and pepper for good measure.

In a place where service is desultory, these seasonings arrive promptly and I enjoy my tepid tucker. The wine, which is nicely cold, I like much more. It's rich and fruity, but also bone dry. A lovely drink, and I'm quaffing it fast, gulping it as if I've got a whole bottle in front of me (which, as W. C. Fields pointed out, is better than a frontal lobotomy). Interested to know more, I search the label. It's 14.5 per cent alcohol! And I'm guzzling it like mineral water. Soon I'm tremendously contented. Here I am, an atheist of Methodist upbringing in a Muslim museum nearing Christmas, the happiest day of the Christian year. Everyone around me seems reposed and cheerful, too; smiles beaming. Even the grossly overweight American couple four benches along are finding Paris exhilerating. She's reading to him from a guidebook. They are agog at the treats they're about to experience.

In a few minutes, I'll stroll by the Seine through the Tino Rossi garden, which commemorates an actor and singer said to be the most famous Corsican after Napoleon. During my first Christmases in France there was always a moment — after the turkey with chestnut stuffing — when one of my sisters-in-law, usually Bénédicte, the youngest, clamoured for Tino Rossi to be 'put on'. What 'went on' the turntable was a sweetly crooned rendition of his most famous song, *Petit Papa Noël*. He first recorded it in 1946, and in a very short time it sold tens of millions of copies worldwide. And, although Tino Rossi died in 1983 in his seventies, he and his song still sell thousands of copies a year.

In the run-up to the Christmases of the early 1970s, I remember Tino being invited on to every variety show on French television. The hosts and viewers wanted only one song — *Petit Papa Noël*. The ballad is exemplarily saccharine, but Tino did have a lovely light tenor. It begins with an introduction that sets the scene of a '*belle nuit de Noël*'. Snow has spread its white overcoat (I'm translating direct here), children are urged to say a final prayer before a sandman weighs heavily on their eyelids, and then comes the refrain:

*Petit Papa Noël*
*Quand tu descendras du ciel*
*Avec des jouets par milliers*
*N'oublie pas mon petit soulier.*

Little Father Christmas, it says, when you come down from the sky with your thousands of toys don't forget my little shoe. (Christmas presents are stacked against French children's shoes.)

It's silly, trite and consumerist, but it has become a synecdoche for the warmth and love with which I — a funny foreigner — was embraced by a French family all those years ago. By my wife-to-be-then-wife, of course. But also by a mother-in-law who had lost her husband to cancer at forty-eight. Who got up at dawn for the rest of her life to continue running the butcher's shop. Who handled the money. Who made sure Marcel, the shop's *chef*, went to the market, bought the meat and broke it down correctly, managed the apprentice and maintained the business. Who ensured that he was well looked after in return for his labours. Who kept her clients, including Salvador Dali, satisfied with the range and quality of her produce. Who brought up a gaggle of wonderful daughters and a son while she ran the shop. And, what with the reminiscences, the taste of chestnut stuffing in my mouth, a light spicy whiff of couscous in my nostrils and the words of *Petit Papa Noël* scrolling in some of the deepest veins of my memory, Tino's renowned voice clear, his diction perfect, and the Lebanese rosé — let's not forget the Lebanese rosé — going down a treat, I start weeping. Within seconds, I'm crying bucketloads. Not sobbing — no convulsions — but I am weeping rather heavily. I cover my face with my handkerchief and blow my nose. Nothing works, and I sit back, sip the rosé, let the emotion overwhelm me, remember, and cry my heart out.

In the Tino Rossi garden, which borders the river, I can't find a plaque or bust of the great man. But it's about four hundred metres long and fifty wide and I'd be surprised if there weren't some recognition somewhere. The sun penetrates heavy cloud for a second or two every quarter-hour. The air, clear and cold, smells faintly manured and icy. Constructed a few metres above river level, the garden itself must be relatively recent. It's a spacious mixture of paved areas, swirling rockeries, shrubs, specimen trees, grassy knolls and steps down to the quayside, here called the Port Saint-Bernard. Quite a few pedestrians are out strolling. The river in this part of town seems a little wider, the city more spacious, the buildings on either side less imposing. Tino Rossi's garden could be a river-park virtually anywhere. London, say, by the lower Thames. It's good for my composure.

I head upstream, taking an exit from Tino's garden outside the very much larger, classical and alleyed Jardin des Plantes. I have in mind a particular pilgrimage — to the Gare d'Austerlitz. It's only a few hundred metres and I'm there quickly. In recent years, Austerlitz, the protagonist of W. G. Sebald's eponymous novel, and the station itself have garnered a small amount of fame. Sebald's Austerlitz had the idea that his father left Paris from this station soon after the Germans entered the city. He envisaged his father leaning out of the window of his compartment, 'and I saw the white clouds of smoke rising from the locomotive as it began to move ponderously away'. It was, Austerlitz thought, the 'most mysterious of all the railway terminals of Paris'. He was fascinated by the way Métro trains roll over the iron viaduct 'into the station's upper storey, quite as if the facade were swallowing them up'. He was also entranced by the immense gabled curtain of glass — held intact by ornate ironwork — that hangs above the far end of the platforms.

But, although it's a theme that resonates through this great book, Austerlitz failed to note the station's darkest aspect: the block capitals that are chiselled into a massive, white marble plaque on the western wall. From this station on 14 May 1941, says the stone, 3700 Jewish men were deported to their deaths at Auschwitz. Furthermore, between 19 and 22 July 1942, 7800 Jews, including 4000 children, were consigned to Auschwitz — and death — from this station. Signed by a group called the 'sons and daughters of deported French Jews', the inscription finishes, 'Let us never forget'.

In the station's bookshop I buy an intensely moving paperback. It's the story of Coluche's charity, '*Les restaurants du coeur*'. Not the full story — just the first twenty years. Coluche was the funniest man in France in the early 1980s. Millions listened to his radio show on Europe 1. His stand-up seasons in big venues sold out. He wore a t-shirt, blue-and-white striped overalls and ludicrous shoes in canary-yellow. I have one of his LPs. In a strong Parisian accent that bent and smeared vowels and consonants into a sometimes jokey, sometimes lugubrious, whine, he'd complain equally about *flics* and hitch-hikers, the government, bureaucrats and hoons, punctuating it with outrageous little ditties. He never forgot his origins — how could he?

In the 1950s, Michel Colucci was the son of poor Italian immigrants in a southern Parisian suburb. His father died

young, and his mother, a florist, did what she could to bring
up her family. In the toughest times, Michel dreamt of a world
where those who had lots of money shared it with those who
had none. Silly boy! Then he became Coluche of the corrosive
humour, a prince of subversive satire, with comments like:
'When I was little in our house the hardest times were the end
of the month. Especially the last thirty days.' And: 'If there are
blokes who have money and are pissed off because it doesn't
bring them happiness they only need say so: we'll always find
poor people stupid enough to steal it from them.'

Coluche became very rich. Simultaneously, he became
concerned. So concerned, in fact, about the state of French
politics that he attempted to run for President in 1981. Then,
on 26 September 1985, he'd had enough, and wondered aloud
on Europe 1 if anyone was interested in sponsoring a canteen
in Paris — and later in other big French cities — that would
serve two or three thousand free meals a day to the city's poor
and destitute. I have a strong feeling that I've heard a
recording of this, now famous, public daydream that was
stated partly in an off-hand manner but also with a sense of
urgency. The ball was rolling.

To establish *Les restos du coeur* (restaurants of the
heart), as Coluche called them, took an immense amount
of perserverance in the face of bureaucratic hurdles the
height of Everest. But with a group of powerful friends,
and by brilliant use of the media, he vaulted them. Ordinary
French people donated millions of francs, and the first
*resto* distributed food in joyful chaos on 21 December — less
than three months after his original musing. Very quickly
every man, woman and child in France was aware of
the *restos*, and Coluche himself was surpised that his
'silly little idea', as he called it, had become an enormous
project. Six months later — after a successful first winter
'season' — Coluche was killed when his motorbike and a
truck collided near Cannes. You will find some Frenchmen

today who still think it was a conspiracy. Coluche was murdered, they'll tell you. He was too embarrassing for the French who rule. A recent poll ranked him the fifth greatest man of Gaul.

Today, *Les Restaurants du Coeur* and *Les Relais du Coeur* constitute France's biggest charity. Some 470,000 donors contributed 41 million euros in money or kind to the 2004–2005 winter campaign, with 45,000 aid workers distributing 67 million meals. The organisations put roofs over 2700 heads, had 95 food trucks on the roads and organised 755 cultural events and amusements. Coluche would have loved it. But I shouldn't be reading this modest history in the Métro's busy line four. Page 189 tips me over. It's blank apart from a single quote from Coluche. I suspect it's from one of his stand-up routines: halfway through, probably, when the audience would be screaming with laughter. There'd be silence while he sniggered and shouted in his flat Parisian smear, *'Maaaais ouuuuuuuiiii!'* More silence. Laughter. A snigger. 'My most important project?' He'd fire the words like rockets into the theatre's blackness. Silence. 'To continue living!' Uproar. Guffaws. And I am crying again.

—

My niece Magali lives not far from me above the boulevard. Her apartment is on the fifth floor, no lift. (It's what the French call a don't-forget-the-bread apartment.) It's smaller than mine but charming, and in it she not only carries on her day-to-day life but works as a freelance graphic designer. Of less — or more, depending on your gender — importance, is that she is approaching thirty (most people think she looks about nineteen) and has the usual 'men' problems of woman her age. She is petite and gorgeous, with long, honey-blonde hair and chestnut eyes. And that very special untouchable-touchable golden skin.

We meet on the median strip at the top of the stairs above Anvers Métro station. She apologises for being five minutes late. Who couldn't accept it? She's smiling sweetly, rugged-up and gloved, and wearing a pink knitted bonnet with a big rosette. (Bonnets are huge this winter.) We're off to the other side of town to eat at a steak restaurant that comes highly recommended. Then we have tickets to Paris's sexiest cabaret, Le Crazy Horse.

I love spending time with Maggie (or Maggie Wheels, or Mag Wheels, as we call her in Australia, after the magnesium-alloy wheels that go on hot cars). She and I can hug and go arm-in-arm in the street and it thrills me when people look at us — Parisian minds are easily read. Mag Wheels looks so young, and I'm realising with pain that I'm a senior — if a junior one. The Métro warms her to an important topic. She'd love to find a husband and have children, but the men she has dated in recent years — and the one she is dating now — are never ready to settle into monogamy and fatherhood. They don't want to be responsible for bringing up kids. There are too many more exciting things a young man can do these days. I can add nothing except sympathy, agreeing with her right down the line. When I was young, I say, it was fashionable — the done thing — to be partnered up to the hilt and mortgaged even further. And to change nappies. It was what people did. Nowadays, that brand of enrichment is *passé*.

Le Severo is a tiny place, luxuriously panelled in french-polished timbers. Bare hardwood tables are many, small and close. Indeed, one particular table for two hugs a pillar: somebody would need to eat round the corner, so to speak. Maggie and I are first in, followed quickly by two women and a man — proper senior Parisians.

Two fellows in chefs' tunics and a more casual chap, who stubs out a cigarette, finish a conversation at a rear table. They bid *au revoir*, the out-of-uniform fellow leaving with a brief '*bon soir*' to all of us. The neater and tidier of the chef-suited gents adopts a genial-host role, greeting us all with a welcome and a smile. The other retreats to what must be a tiny kitchen behind the bar.

Monsieur Front-of-House is, indeed, the boss — he makes this clear to us from what he says about the produce. We all stand around two blackboards empanelled in a wall. In white-chalked capitals, one lists the menu, the other the wine. The boss seems an odd sort of cook, or even restaurant-owner: he looks like a retired history teacher with his steel-rimmed glasses and greying, college-cut hair. I tell him Le Severo was recommended by a certain restaurateur. He's delighted, he says. They share butchers. Actually, their butcher is the chap who just left. We're in for a great beefy treat, he assures us. He recommends anything on the list, but the *côte de boeuf* (beef chop) is formidable and huge. He sits us at a tiny round table. The other customers are sent far away to the other side of the room — at least three metres distant.

Heavy maroon drapes hang from brass rails halfway up windows. Terribly traditional. And there are benches or timber bistro chairs with elegantly inlaid backs and seats. Big white, worked fabric napkins catch your dribbles, and Le Severo's cutlery is excellent — forks are old and classically shaped, and the knives have bone handles and keen edges.

Above us the blackboards announce entrées of Auvergne ham, slices of 'rosette' salami from the same area, leeks with a vinaigrette sauce, and a salad starring fresh goats' cheese, all costing from 6 to 10 euros. For mains you can order *steak haché* (hamburger) and chips for 14 euros, steak tartare with chips for 15 euros, beef fillet for 25 euros and a *côte* for two or three people (65 or 75 euros). There are perhaps forty wines listed, many of them costing in the twenties of euros.

Le Severo's produce *is* wonderful: the rillettes rich, fatty and porky, the ham perfumed. Hand-cut chips are excellent and the *côte* has come from an enormous beast with marvellous flavour. It's been just sealed on the outside. The interior flesh is maroon and bloody raw, oozing juices. Just the way I like it. We drink a rich and fruity 2004 Morgon made by Jean-Paul Thévenet. From gamay grapes, it costs 28 euros.

Constantly cutting slices off big loaves of a terrific, crusty sourdough, the boss is never still. Until he takes a breather with us. He's William Bernet, he says, and his chef, Johnny Beguin, has been with him since 1987. He tugs at his tunic. He's not a chef at all. He used to be a butcher, but Le Severo has become his life — so successful lately that he's changing nothing, only enlarging the operation. He opened a new place, Le Bis du Severo (Severo B, if you like), only three months ago, installing a Japanese cook who does an interesting take on traditional Gallic dishes.

There's a pause, before Magali, in all innocence, throws a gastronomic grenade. Can she have some mustard, please, to go with the beef? William gulps. Mustard? You'd like mustard? Now, I have a view on this, I say, intervening hurriedly. I suggest to William, the butcher who isn't a chef, that if you run a steak restaurant you should do more than present bloody brilliant meat on a plate. Or even bloody brilliant meat and commercial mustards on a plate. Does he remember Le Relais de Venise, near Porte Maillot, where people queued in winter for the privilege of eating? Thirty years ago, you ate at the Relais not because of the high quality of the meat, although that was important, but because of its 'secret' house sauce. Every steak restaurant should have one. You build it on a base of great brown sauce, I say. William smiles politely but shakes his head. He clearly can't agree.

'Do you really want mustard with meat like that?' he asks Magali.

Maggie Wheels says yes, she would prefer her steak with some Dijon, please. William smiles and shakes his head again, looks at us a little ruefully and takes three steps into the kitchen.

'And she's a butcher's daughter, as well,' I shout after him. 'And granddaughter!'

I'm dying to know the answer. What does a contemporary girl do about her brazilian in polite company? It's all right for most women, who undress only with intimates. But what about the girls of Le Crazy Horse, Paris's most famous nude spectacle? They're very beautiful, their bodies the last word in the female physique. I suspect that being modern, cool and super-sexy — the sort of girls who could pull boyfriends and partners from Paris's most celebrated and wealthiest ranks — they'd also be *à la page* in grooming. If I understand women these days — and the jury is clearly still out on that — this means they'll be waxed to the ultimate follicle. But will Le Crazy, which has been known for more than half-a-century for displaying complete nudity or '*nu intégral*', expose twenty-first-century women's plucked pudenda?

Maggie and I pick up complimentary tickets at the box office. (Le Crazy has invited me.) The theatre is much smaller than the Lido but much bigger than I remember it. From two previous visits long ago, I recall only blackness and babes. Goings-on in a cave. Having left Methodism behind, I devoured each show. The second visit had its consequences, though: Dominique and I had bumped into a wonderful old friend from my former church and one of his colleagues. They'd been in Paris doing some work for a big chain-link fencing company, had finished their business a day early and were, for twenty-four hours, tourists. We had time off, so we showed them around. My friend Jeff, who was level-headed, a great man and mentor and a somewhat unconventional Methodist in that he was unafraid of fun, mentioned in passing a curious coincidence: their boss and his wife were holidaying in Paris. They didn't particularly want to look them up. Naturally, I said. But as we walked up the rue Tronchet towards the department stores, Mr and Mrs Managing Director headed towards us from the opposite direction. Much back-slapping and laughing at the smallness of the world.

'What are you doing tonight, boys?' asked the MD, and Jeff turned to me. What *could* they do? A show? Something really typical of Paris? Really *Parisian*! Dominique and I thought fast. You've got to understand that, by then, I'd become almost a native. I'd forgotten about prudishness, for which there *is* a French word, but not one you'd ever hear. In the 1970s Australians were still in many ways cultural adolescents — supporters of self-important and ultra-conservative Judeo-Christian politicians, bureacracies and institutions. (In many ways, we still haven't grown up: see the institutional and political pressure on abortion, or our poor public transport policies yet simultaneous obsession with the road toll.) And I suggested Le Crazy. Wonderful, said Mr MD. Look, I said, it's a bit rude, and the girls are nude... Completely. Mrs MD looked stern. The boys pricked up their ears. But, I said, there are also great non-girlie acts — magicians, contortionists and so on. Just brilliant. 'Great,' said Mr MD, smiling broadly. 'Sounds terrific. I'll book the tickets, and it's my shout!' Mrs MD grimaced.

We all turned up, sat in the dark with our drinks, and the show began. I looked along the row. The boys were loving it. Mr MD appeared to be trying to love it, but from time to time I noticed him patting his wife's hand. And her face! Set. Granite. Probably insulted. Appalled. Certainly very, very offended.

As we left the theatre, the boys and Mr MD all told me how much they'd loved Le Crazy. Especially the girls. Great choice. So artistic. Jeff put an arm around my shoulder and told me not to worry. The boss's wife would get over it. He could tell me this out loud because Mrs MD was well out of earshot. She was striding up the middle of the avenue George V — it was late at night, so no traffic — four metres away. She was putting a respectable distance, you see, between herself and men who enjoyed filth. (Dominique stuck with us.) When they got back to the hotel, Mr MD was going to get the earful of his life. I never heard, by the way, if he did.

Has the world changed? Australia has, of course, but not enough. And I suppose that, if I'd had a beautiful young French niece back then, I could have sat in Le Crazy Horse with her and nobody — certainly neither she nor I — would have thought there was anything odd or salacious in it. On the contrary, Maggie is tonight looking forward to the staging, lighting and production values. It will be a treat for her graphic eye.

We're led to wide bench seats towards the back of the theatre in very plush blood-red velour. Not too far behind us is the bar, from which you can watch the performance for 49 euros. In the stalls it's 90 euros and, for your money, you get two alcoholic drinks in huge glass tumblers. Both my *gin-tonics*, as they call them in France, are among the most powerful I've swallowed. Wonderful.

Dubbed Taboo, the *spectacle* begins with an ensemble piece, the twenty girls undressed militaristically — saucy grenadiers. Their choreography is fast, snappy and in perfect unison. The lighting is fabulous — fast, furious, soft, dazzling, laminated, etiolated and shimmering. At times it flares on the dancers' exemplary forms, at others it fretworks them. It makes the Lido's efforts look second-rate. Katcha Kiev, Lasso Calypso, Misty Flashback, Nooka Karamel,

Wendy Window, Psykko Tico, Yodel Weiss, Xya Cyclamen, Athena Perfecto, Lady Pousse-Pousse and their colleagues are breathtakingly precise, their high-stepping poker straight, their costumes (and lack of them) stylish and original. Recorded music is funky and loud.

Since its 1951 launching by former painter and antique dealer Alain Bernardin, Le Crazy has dedicated itself to what it calls 'the art of the nude'. In *Paris by Night* there is a photograph of Monsieur Bernardin. Perhaps in his late thirties, he has sharp handsome features and is dressed in a fine suit and check silk tie. There isn't much of his own neatly coiffed, fair, straight hair, but he holds the tumbling, curly mane of a Brigitte-Bardot-lookalike who is sucking her right thumb. Perhaps in envy or astonishment (the girl is wearing nothing more than a tiny bikini bottom), his eyes bulge. The book calls Bernardin 'Monsieur Strip-Tease in person', a man who had 'vision enough to introduce strip-tease *in toto* into French Night Life' and its author, Jacques Robert, writes that Monsieur Bernardin looks like a young man of good family. He was, in fact, expelled from a convent school for 'working on rather tasteful "indecent" drawings' (and is quoted as saying that 'it isn't feasible to maintain that a nude woman is indecent'). Believe it if you care to, but apparently Bing Crosby suggested the idea of the Crazy Horse to Alain Bernardin — the club was supposed to be a 'very realistic flashback of the brash Western saloons of the 1870s'. What I'm seeing, though, has not the remotest connection to cowboys, Indians, masked men, silver bullets, Zorro, Gene Autry or Hopalong Cassidy.

And my question is answered almost immediately. No naked pudenda. The girls wear tiny pubic hair patches. I lean over to Maggie Wheels: 'They've got wigs on.' But, of course, she says, giggling.

Vik & Fabrini, a double-act of staggeringly clever magicians, and Les Blackwits, weird caterpillar and butterfly puppets that tell intellectual sight gags at lightspeed, perform mute. But it's the girls who win, and singly, doubly or *en ensemble* they are sublime. I seem to recall that, thirty-odd years ago, the scenes, which followed in quick succession, were more blatantly erotic. Today's are suavely suggestive and technically very, very impressive. Only the narrowest of Western minds could find them offensive. And, for a reason other than the slickness of the production and the ideas she's taken from it, Maggie Wheels is gleeful. She grabs my elbow as we leave. Smiling broadly, she thanks her *tonton* (uncle) for inviting her and adds, 'I saw some cellulite!'

# day eleven

Mag Wheels often does her laps in the Georges Drigny pool in the rue Bochart-de-Saron, just off the boulevard. She can't swim this morning, she tells me when I ring. She has work to do (I wonder if it's a hangover from the excitement of seeing a Crazy girl with cellulite). But I need to exercise before tackling lunch at one of Paris's most historic and expensive (I've been invited) restaurants, Ledoyen. Is it still the 'leader' of Parisian gastronomy? I'll know by mid-afternoon.

I pay my 2.60 euros, ask for directions to the changing room, and pass a huge salad bowl containing a sugarloaf of metal washers. There's a notice on a piece of cardboard jabbed into the pile. In black marker pen it reads, '*Jetons deux euros*'. I can't imagine why a washer worth a few cents would cost two euros. I should have thought about it more deeply.

You descend to the pool here, too, but not as far as in the rue Rochechouart. I'm ignorant of the ropes, expecting someone to take my clothes from me in return for a numbered bracelet, but the routine is different, with banks of battleship-grey lockers confronting me. You need to put two euros in a slot on the inside of the locker door to close it.

At least, that's what a notice says. But neither a two-euro coin nor two one-euro coins fit and I can't shut the door. A dangerously thin man with snow-coloured skin shivers on a three-rung bench a little way from me. In silence he holds up one of the washers from the salad bowl at reception. He's offering it to me. I'm confused, but I take it. It works, fitting the slot inside the door to the millimetre. I turn to the chap who offered it.

'What about the two euros?' I say, fumbling among coins. He waves a hand. I insist. He won't take the money. I wonder why. Two euros is not an insignificant sum. I close the locker, hoping I can remember my four-digit code.

The pool is eerily similar to the one I visited last week. Think Parisian pools and you see stern lifeguards, powder-blue and white walls, wet tiled floors and people of all ages and sexes sharing the showers. You hear the same caveman echoes here as you do at pools the world over. Kids yelp and bray, and the sounds of splashing and occasional pea-whistles are an obbligato to a ground bass of enormous filtration equipment rumbling away somewhere below.

This pool is as crowded as last week's and I struggle to complete a worthwhile tally of laps. In the two lanes reserved for earnest swimmers, only one person shows any real form. She's young and tumble-turning at the ends. Nice style, too, even if her strokes cross her body a little too much when they enter the water. I point this out to her as she takes a breather, expecting a response less abrupt than I'd get in Australia.

'OK,' she says, thanking me in a thick accent. She's from Chile, she reveals, and she's studying psychology here for a couple of months. Why Paris? To learn French. But also for the prestige of studying in France. Hmmmm, I say. Did she consider Australia? She would have learnt a language that's in many ways more useful.

She stares hard at me, pulls her goggles over her eyes, and kicks off up the pool. She's crossing her strokes more than ever. Eccentrically. Determinedly.

Back in the changing-room, everyone is reclaiming their two-euro *jetons* from the locker doors. (Not too long ago, you used to have to buy smaller *jetons* from tobacconists to make a public phone work.) I take mine back to the reception and toss it into the salad bowl.

'You don't really charge two euros for those, do you?' I say to the girl behind the counter.

'Of course not,' she says.

———

I suggest you overcome your spluttering attack upon noticing that Ledoyen's specialities are priced between 82 and 95 euros, and turn instead to a fascinating narrative. The restaurant's history is on the back of the *carte*. It's headed, 'Ledoyen, two hundred years of Parisian life' (my translation).

Pierre-Michel Doyen was the son of caterers and set up his restaurant on the Champs Elysées in 1791. The revolutionaries Robespierre, Danton and Marat were all clients of what one contemporary observer described as a small, white house with green shutters and a merry-go-round with wooden horses in its garden. Napoléon and Joséphine met here, so the story goes. In 1814, it more or less officially took on its owner's name, becoming a great Parisian *table*. It was notable, according to one restaurant guide, for its prompt service. Whether it wasn't fast enough when it came to steak tartare is not mentioned, but a camp of cossacks destroyed the restaurant — and other nearby buildings — soon after.

A new 'Pavillon Ledoyen' was built off the Champs in 1842, amid chestnut and willow trees, lawns and fountains. And it was much-loved, even if it became known as a lunch-spot for short-fused *racailles* about to fight duels. In time, it became popular with artists such as Degas, Manet and Monet, and writers — Zola, Flaubert and Guy de Maupassant among them. During dinner at Ledoyen, André Gide founded France's most influential literary magazine and publishing firm, the Nouvelle Revue Française. For several years following the war it was officially a venue for French foreign-office receptions, and it re-opened as a privately owned restaurant only in 1962. Since then, says the back cover, it has become a renowned rendezvous for politicians and the 'grand' Parisian bourgeoisie.

Irrespective of its background, Ledoyen is an unusual restaurant in the French capital. First, it's the only one with such a long history — all the others that opened in post-revolutionary France, at the dawn of the modern restaurant era, including Méot, Beauvilliers, Les Provençaux, Mme Hardy, Rocher de Cancale and Véry, are no more. Secondly, it remains a pavilion among mature trees, lawns and gardens, something of an achievement in a city where rebuilding is constant.

From the outside, Ledoyen today is a sizeable but elegant two-storey building painted a mustard colour — more hot English than Dijon, oddly enough. Inside, the opulence begins immediately, and I'm asked to wait in a kind of spacious downstairs sitting room for a few moments before being shown up a broad staircase to the dining room.

Patrick Simiand welcomes me at the top of the stairs. He remembers my visits to Mietta's in Melbourne, where he was on the floor for two years during the 1980s. Ledoyen's director (the modern title for a maitre d') possesses the kind of easy charm that seems to come naturally to top hospitality-industry people. Tall, with wire-rimmed glasses, he is sobrely suited. Flamboyance is the last thing you need from service staff in a great restaurant. The food and the wine *must* do the talking.

No distractions. It's one of the things people like Patrick know only too well.

But I am distracted immediately by the large rectangular dining room itself. (Mind you, ambience becomes less diverting over time.) It's rich from the carpet up. The windows are hung with maroon velvet drapes so heavy they could stop birdshot. The patterned carpet is thick, and the original 1840s ceiling is intricate — its fine floral swirls, bordered by rectangles, triangles and arcs of filligreed gold, suggest the formal gardens of a great French palace. Knife handles look as if they're made from solid silver, and the huge palest apricot napkins are embroidered with 'Ledoyen'. Here is complete, classic luxury.

But the overall impression is not one of nineteenth-century overload. Other eras have obviously intruded, and the result, while quite homogeneous, is a little old-fashioned. A verdant climbing plant is here, mauve Singapore orchids there. Hefty mahogany caddies of perhaps late-Victorian or even twentieth-century persuasion contain champagnes and alcohols. Despite the original ceiling, there's a fair bit of feinting with the later and the new.

I am a little surprised — but perhaps shouldn't be — by Ledoyen's guests, who, all but one, arrive after me. Tables, I should add, are so widely separated that no business confidences, let alone personal ones, are likely to be overheard.

Some three metres to my left are two large and senior gentlemen who might (not long ago) have captained certain motors of the French commercial machine. Or even played roles in its politics, although I don't recognise them. Wrapped in jackets and waistcoats, they are at tremendous ease, and perhaps once earned enough to buy this place. Far away in the top corner, the three who have just arrived could quite easily do so now. Then they'd sell, I suspect, finding the going too hard for the return involved. They're two men and a woman in their late thirties or early forties. Fashion or rock music, I'd guess. One of the men wears cuban heels, tight jeans and an expansive jacket of red and yellow stripes. Several metres of orange gauze are wound around his throat. The second man is completely in black apart from charcoal-grey suede shoes. The woman is Asian, high-booted, her body lost in layers of taupe-coloured clothes with more cut than a theatre critic. They talk loudly, showing us all that this is their canteen.

Then there are the two youngish blokes who are *really* at home at Ledoyen. Born to be here, in fact. No airs needed. They are from noble families, their supple grey trousers, razor-sharp creases, demur silk ties and tweed jackets say. They know the waiters and exchange *bons mots*. They smile and laugh (although how anyone can smile or laugh knowing what they are about to pay for this lunch is beyond me). And finally a Japanese couple in their early twenties sit across the room, as watchful as two moggies in the sun.

Over the next couple of hours I experience the highest of high French eating. Ledoyen is similar to Taillevent, there's no denying, but there are also differences, with Ledoyen creating a slightly more formal experience. It plates smaller servings of fussier food. To differentiate themselves, the three-star restaurants have only one route to take in this era of casualness — towards ever more finicky formality and gastronomic sophistication. That's how they stand apart from the brasseries and bistros that reproduce classic French dishes of varying quality. Ledoyen delivers altitudinal refinement — the kinds of flavours and textures you have to search for. And there is originality here, too, even if it's restrained.

Four sorts of freshly baked breads are offered with wonderful salty butter. Then a silver salver of palate-teasers. There are two globes of a seafood mousse so light that I'm surprised they don't levitate to the ceiling. Each wears a two-millimetre square flake of dried seaweed that must have been posed with tweezers. Inside the foam is a morsel of langoustine tail. Two small bricks of foie gras mousse are contained between tanned wafers so thin and brittle that I half-expect them to crack as I pick them up. There are little blocks of seafood jelly with crystalline caps, and two minute, super-crisp and very tasty spring rolls. And then the real food begins.

First out is a beetroot medley, the root in different forms stacked above a block of tiny bits of smoked eel and aromatic vegetables in an emulsion. A thin square of the vegetable separates the eel from microscopic beetroot cubes in a dressing. A glistening dome of beetroot sabayon tops the lot like the roof of a sports stadium. That's beetroot, more beetroot, and beetroot yet again. Do not ask to hold the beetroot. The eel pieces are quite salty, but there's no doubting the kitchen's technical skills. Nor the time it must take to prepare something so worked.

Just as showy is a sea-urchin concoction. Perhaps the egg sacs of a whole urchin (or possibly even a couple) have been plundered for this dish. Some two dozen long thin tongues of brilliant orange roe are arranged over an avocado mousse in a mauve urchin shell. Atop the swirl of egg sacs is a soufflé of scallop roe in paler orange. The shell itself is steadied in a conical glass dish by small coffee-coloured ovoids of glass. Tastes are good but a little faint, and I'm noticing again that French restaurant food is saltier than I'm used to.

My third true starter is a ripper. As if riding in a gondola, two balls of baby lobster tail sit above more crustacean tailflesh in its shell. Around the balls has been wound a hair-fine North African 'macaroni', which is deep-fried and tanned. Between the two is an oozing sludge of off-white — just faintly green-tinged — emulsion that comprises hazelnut oil and herbs of several sorts. Of transcendental deftness, this dish really works. It's great because of the superb balance of sweet savours. None is lost, despite their slightness.

My first main is a Ledoyen speciality (three are listed, following six entrées, four fish dishes and six of meat). It's a small block of very white-fleshed turbot, caught by line — not netted. It's a witty construction, because the alabaster top of the block appears to have been seared on a barbecue grill. With some precision, too. But the black grill marks are nothing of the kind. I'm told they're composed of ground, dried truffle that solidifies into a thin plaque. The fish sits on crushed potatoes in an off-white froth. Flavours are again delicate and very refined, the sweet mustiness of truffles invading my nostrils. Placed between the phantom grill-bars, three pale yellow-green leaves the size of nailheads — they're from celery tops — garnish the fish.

My second main is a single enormous sweetbread, a tawny neck gland from a vealer. It's nut-brown, its surface significantly caramelised. Two short sticks of lemongrass penetrate the gland at right angles, going in one side and coming out the other. It's Saint Sebastian and the arrows, a martyr of a dish. The sweetbread sits on a raft of thin salsify batons in a bright-green *jus* composed from eight herbs and butter. The result is exquisite, the sweetbread flesh claggy, sweet and flavoursome, its lemongrass skewers lending the faintest of inscrutable tastes.

Desserts maintain the standard: a pineapple sludge wears the lightest meringue possible; and a major construction of sesame wafers, pistachio ice cream and warm melting chocolate oozing into a fine nest of something indefinable but sweet should be magnified a million times so that the girls at Le Crazy can dance through it.

I am regaled with a different drink — almost always wine — for each course. They are all wonderful; the kinds of liquid treasures that only the greatest restaurants can afford these

days. There's a 'yellow' wine like a fino sherry with conté
cheese. And a very special cider with my camembert. A
Viognier escorted the sweetbread, and the 1996 hundred-per-
cent chardonnay champagne with which I began the meal is
the best bubbly I've drunk. (It's from Jacquesson, a small
maker, dates from 1996, and Ledoyen sells it for 90 euros
a bottle. Mind you, only three thousand cases are produced a
year.) A dark and pharmaceutical 'Maydie' wine partners the
chocolate dessert.

Ledoyen lists no Australian wines, even though the
sommelier, Géraud Tournier, tells me he loves them. He has
twice driven from Adelaide to Melbourne, sipping here and
there. He raves about Jasper Hill. Why no antipodean wines
on the list, then? He explains. I understand the commercial
technicalities of the wine trade less than well, but it has
something to do with the distribution of imported wines
within Paris and the reliability of supplies.

And soon the chef himself, a thin, big-boned Breton, is
out and about, visiting the tables. I congratulate Christian Le
Squer on his food. But what about the Senderens contention
that French cooking is slipping behind? He draws breath and
pauses quite a long time before replying.

'You know,' he says, 'we eat well in France and our
cooking is still at a pretty unbeatable level.'

I don't disagree, eschewing yet another debate about
letting loose the 'unbeatable', laudable and obvious skills of
French cooks on a wider range of ingredients. We wish each
other well, and he moves across to the young Japanese. I
notice shiny stone-washed jeans and black runners under his
voluminous white tunic and apron.

Patrick Simiand shows me out, asking for news of
Melbourne. I get him up to speed as best I can. He wants to
know what Monsieur A and Madame B are doing; if I've seen
them lately. We touch briefly on the very big difference
between the best French and Australian cooking. I laud

Ledoyen's enormous finesse and its partnerings of drinks and dishes. In Australia, as well he knows, I say, ingredients are less worked, and the trick is to balance several of them in more natural states on the plate. Here, the emulsions and froths have their own constructed genius. But they also produce far less aggressive flavours. In the New World, I laugh, we specialise in culinary *matériel* — taste incendiaries. Mouth explosives.

I intend to visit or revisit a museum. Perhaps the Picasso or Marmottan-Monet. Or even the Musée d'Orsay, where I had a very ordinary lunch in an extravagant room of sun-king decor with Maggie Wheels and my wife during a recent trip. But as I envelop myself to re-enter the fridge sometimes known as the Champs Elysées, I realise walking at a fairly stiff pace — and continuing to walk — will be a better option.

I cross the place de la Concorde and its *obélisque*, watching out for fast-moving cars, whose rumbling over the cobbles luckily warns of their approach. Through the Tuileries gardens I go, through the Louvre courtyard, then north, up to the Palais Royal and its arcaded antique garden, classy couture boutiques and art dealers.

Nothing has changed here since the days when I took meal-breaks from Agence France-Presse. I hope nothing ever will. You can walk like this for hours in Paris, never beginning with a specific route or even a direction, and you will never be bored. (As it happens, it looks as if I'm heading home.) Hemingway said that if 'you are lucky enough to have lived in Paris as a young man, then wherever you go for the rest of your life, it stays with you...' He was right, scoring a bull's-eye on the matter. Quite banally, I'm churning an emotional feast. But I'm also turning over a physical one. I don't feel at all uncomfortably full, luckily, but I won't eat out tonight.

For a few francs — on recollection, a little over four — in the 1970s you were served a four-course meal at the Agence France-Presse canteen. You began with salads, terrines or *crudités* (sliced and dressed raw vegetables), moved along to a 'wet' dish, usually a stew or roast of some sort, and followed these up with cheese and desserts of various varieties. The dishes were well cooked and tasty, and a quarter-litre of acceptable table wine cost next to nothing. Have things changed? I'm not far from AFP. I'll drop in and find out. It's a bit of a last-resort effort, I'll admit. I sent emails from Australia to try to arrange a meal in the canteen and got no replies.

The agency's headquarters is a stern and incongruous multi-storeyed modernist structure opposite the Grecian classicism of the Paris stock exchange. Whereas you could simply walk into the place years ago, today there are several security doors to negotiate. The glass is so thick it has a bottle-green tinge.

A male and a female — security personnel — are behind a counter in an airlock. He is young and sits at a console of CRT monitors a metre or so from the reception window. She is in early middle-age and fields my inquiry. I recite the short speech I've used several times on this trip: I'm an Australian writer, working on a kind of 'diary *gastronomique*'... Then I take the appropriate branch track. I used to work here thirty years ago. I remember how good the canteen was. I'd like to sample it once again. First, does AFP still have a canteen?

The woman screws up her face and waits several seconds before replying. Yes, she says. Have I organised to visit it? No, I say. I tried. She consults her colleague and returns to me. So you want to eat in the canteen? Yes, I say. She can't do anything. Nothing? Nothing. I should have organised a visit with the head of the English service. Seeing as that's where I worked.

'Can I speak to him?'

'No.'

'Why not?'

'He's gone out.'

'Can I speak to someone on the English desk?'

By this stage, I'm irritating the woman. She doesn't need a mid-afternoon confrontation with a gastronomic diarist. She'd rather be doing her crossword. She regards me with contempt and picks up a phone. She turns her back and whispers into it. I can't hear what she is saying. She passes me the handpiece. An affable young chap with a South African accent says hello. I explain my plight. Look, he says, he's on a deadline and has to file a story about Ethiopia. It's on the screen in front of him. He's right up against it. Very sorry, but the best thing he can suggest is for me to go direct to the head of the English service. He gives me his name and number.

I go home, trying the *chef du service anglais* repeatedly throughout the afternoon. I fail to reach him. I leave messages, but nobody from the English service — let alone its boss — gets back to me. *Tant pis,* as the French say. Had someone bothered, the agency might have had well-deserved recognition of how well it looks after its staff, let alone its ability to put out the news.

Surprisingly enough, by eight o'clock I'm hungry. I don't like the look of any of the cafés or restaurants nearby, and I don't feel like Métroing anywhere. Then I remember the camembert I bought more than a week ago. It's in the fridge. When I unwrap it, I find it's in perfect shape — its core of white chalkiness has become smooth, glossy and creamy. I've done a fabulous job maturing it, I tell myself.

I spin down the spiral staircase and walk for all of three hundred metres before finding a little grocery that's still open. It has half-loaves of sourdough in the racks and a selection of three or four new beaujolais. I'm back up the stairs in a trice, and the camembert, the crusty loaf and the fruity red are perfect dinner partners. I'm not at all sure that my meal would pass a dietary analysis, but it's exactly what I feel like eating.

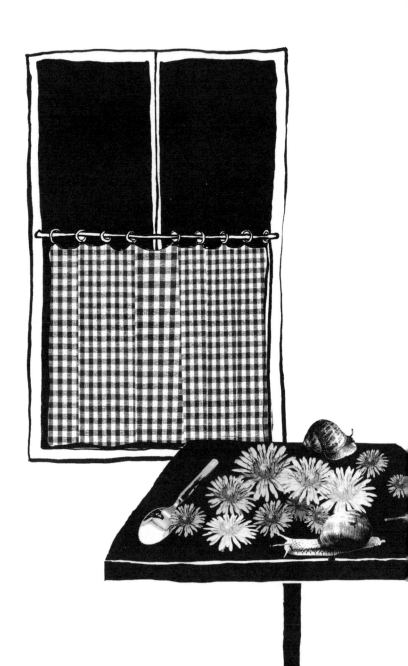

# day twelve

What I'm doing lacks any plausible defence. How dare I write about fabulous food and audacious eating while Africa starves? How dare the French — and the nationals of *all* rich countries — eat well while most of the world's peoples have empty stomachs?

High cooking is an art, we may safely say. But it is an illegitimate one, born out of a desire by those with disgusting wealth and power to push the boundaries of pleasure beyond its more harmless, inclusive and cheap creative manifestations such as dance, music, literature and theatre. It is an art devised by the privileged for their exclusive enjoyment, a pursuit in which the people of the streets cannot participate. Rulers — whether in France, England, Thailand, China or Fiji — sponsored the first and most expensive regal cuisines, because they could afford to do so. As a bonus, eating richly was another way in which they could set themselves above the proletariat.

Today, in Western cities such as Paris, London, Sydney and New York, men and women in finance, commerce, government and law are the new rulers who support contemporary high cooking and keep it exclusive. I fell into writing about food by accident. And not food broadly speaking, of course, but cooking that most Africans and Indians and Asians and South Americans could never taste. Almost three decades later, I am from time to time ashamed of my career. I should chuck it in, I tell myself, become a vegetarian and write about other things. (Many restaurateurs — and so-called colleagues — would be pleased if I did.)

Yet at other times, I remember that I am helping to educate people in my own country to eat more healthily, to consume better and more varied diets, to profit from the simple, enormous and often inexpensive pleasures that cooking brings when we build dishes from raw ingredients. (It's not just a question of tastes and textures but the thrill and satisfaction of creativity.) Moreover, I have identified and revered the chefs and restaurateurs who have democratised eating out in Australia over the past quarter-century. It has been a grand achievement. At least in my home country, almost all people can eat out well from time to time, and the base criterion for every restaurant I test is whether it offers value for money.

All these thoughts are a kind of self-appeasement, and I push on, doing my job, in the hope that the hundreds of millions in Africa and Asia at the other end of eating's very skewed 'normal' curve will one day have enough food in their bellies. More than enough, indeed. And that they will have a diet offering variety as well as satisfying their nutritional needs. It's a challenge I really *should* try to do something about. Musings, these, as I approach the last day of my intensively gourmet fortnight.

<hr />

Aux Lyonnais was — still is — an easy walk from Agence France-Presse. Moreover, it had a Michelin star and was renowned for its hearty renditions of the great culinary classics. Mr Green and his wife were in Paris and wanted to take my wife and me out to dinner. I suggested Aux Lyonnais.

On the chosen date, I could not avoid my shift and would come straight from work, I told them, cribbing a bit of extra time before having to get back to the desk. My wife would come from home and return there — no taxis needed. Lovely, said Mr Green, in that courteous way begat from negotiations over weeks by exchange of handwritten letters. Mr Green, by the way, was no surprise packet disguised as an ordinary man, no reverend from 'Cluedo' or character from an Agatha Christie novel: he was the State of Victoria's top public servant. My father and Mr Green were colleagues and close friends, and Dominique and I, who had heard a little about his toughness and conservatism, had never actually met him. His decisions were straight down the line, my father used to say. He followed the rules and expected others to do likewise. He was the perfect public servant, and a nice man to boot.

So I arrived for dinner at Aux Lyonnais ten minutes late — unintentionally, of course. Dominique was there, as were Mr and Mrs Green. Waiting. At the table. Mr Green was in a pinstripe suit and a club tie. Mrs Green was in a grass-green silk dress, swooping pearls and large earrings. Her light ginger hair had been coiffed into an immaculately towering beehive. They looked magnificent. Spritzy even; they exuded that kind of zest only the freshly scrubbed and impeccably suited can emit.

I remember the roll-neck pullover I was wearing. Its colour, especially. A working-man's colour: shades of diarrhoea. Its sleeves were blackened to the elbows by work. I pushed them up, revealing carbon smears up my forearms. (My hands at least were clean.) I could tell Mr and Mrs Green were shocked. I think they had a higher idea of journalists. They had no notion, at any rate, that someone who made a living from words could be so grubby.

We were all polite to one another, it goes without saying. And I can't remember anything we talked about. The Greens were lovely, but I also think they were dumbfounded,

Mr Green's small eyes frowning too often and for too long at my face. I ate a brilliant *pot au feu,* the boiled meats and leeks tied up with thin string, the accompanying rock salt, gherkins and mustards all excellent. They enjoyed their meals, they said, and went back to their hotel. Dominique went home, and I returned to work. When I got back to the studio at midnight, Dominique had waited up to tell me it was unfortunate that I had arrived at the Lyonnais straight from work. I might have got away with it, she added, if it were not for my moustache. Moustache? I'd never had one. So that's what they had been looking at: my AFP moustache. The heavy black one — in carbon triplicates.

Alain Ducasse recently acquired the Lyonnais, bringing his worldwide stable of tables to twenty-eight, according to one count. Founded in 1890, it's a Bib Gourmand, too, starring 'reactualised' Lyonnais specialities. It is a small high-ceilinged space, with huge mirrors and leafy moulded plaster friezes painted a deep cream. The dado is depicted in wide floral tiles, bordered above and below by green ceramic strips. Below them, reaching to the floor, are white tiles. You sit on deep brown-leather benches or upholstered bistro chairs, and your dark-stained timber table is covered with a wide mat of heavy rough fabric printed with pale red stripes.

The Lyonnais is crowding quickly for lunch. Very businesslike waiters are in shirt sleeves and, when I ask one if I can take a few photographs, he refers me to the manager, who has a short, waxed, brush-backed haircut and wears a fancier shirt with blue stripes and a navy-blue tie. No trouble, he says.

As soon as I sit, small toasted sticks of bread and a bowl of a fresh semi-solid cheese punctuated with chopped herbs and laced with lemon juice is put in front of me. Two suggestions of the 'season' lead off the list: fried scallops with dandelions and beetroot (16 euros), and braised veal cheek (22 euros). Five entrées and the same number of mains follow.

You may order a '*cocotte*' of autumn vegetables for 12 euros or boiled egg with death-trumpet mushrooms and prawns for 15 euros. Among the mains, deer stew comes with vegetables and fruits of the season enhanced with '*lard paysan*', which translates roughly as 'peasant fat'. I have a suspicion there might be some flesh among the fat, and the dish costs 23 euros. Liver from an unweaned vealer with potatoes is priced at 20 euros.

Over the page is the bargain, though: a 28-euro menu of three courses, two choices in each. I take the plate of '*charcuterie lyonnaise*' ahead of the sheep's trotters in a remoulade sauce, the black pudding sausage instead of the quenelle and prawns, and a beaujolais pear with brioche croutons. And, in comparison with starred restaurants, the Lyonnais's wine list is short — three pages that include two champagnes, a beaujolais, seven whites from the Rhône and twenty from Burgundy. Reds are similar in number, and a single rosé precedes a handful of great Lyonnais wines, including a Chevalier-Montrachet 'grand cru' white for 1000 euros.

Slices of crusty brown bread in a grey cheesecloth bag beat my charcuterie platter to the table, but not by long. Actually, the platter is described on the list as a *planche*, or plank. It's of breadboard size, and scattered across it are four sorts of fermented sausage (salami), a slice of pig's-head terrine containing lots of parsley choppings, curls of crispy fried pigskin, and a small bowl of fat warm Ds of classic Lyonnaise pork salami under a gribiche sauce. Halves of small but excellent potatoes, their skins retained, dwell beneath the sausage. The terrine is somewhat salty, but the rest of the spread's components are a sheer delight.

Tables are very close at the Lyonnais, and taking their seats alongside me are two noble French *messieurs* who are perhaps in business together. One wears a chestnut corduroy blazer and the other a V-necked Lacoste pullover of a palette-challenging lemon colour. They comment on the list. One wants to order the Lyonnais's famous *pot au feu* and the other gently chides his friend — 'It's not the season'. They spy the scallops. If only we could get dandelions these days, the chap in the Lacoste jumper says. If we could find only *one*, he emphasises. No question of several.

The black pudding is a surprise. Usually you'll get a single, large blood sausage balancing on a mound of mash. The Lyonnais's is an ice-hockey puck. It's an inch thick and the diameter of a jam-jar lid. And, instead of sitting on mashed potato, it rests on a thick bar of rolled-up macaroni glued together with a bechamel-type sauce. The lot is oiled up and served in a small baking dish of enamelled cast iron. As I look around, all the mains appear to be coming out in these bright orange *cassolettes*.

The gentlemen alongside me are a joy to listen to. Not only does their language flow — their conjugations precise, their nouns sought-for — but they address each other with the polite form of 'you'. Just as at Taillevent, it surprises me. Here are two old friends using a courteous construction. Why they're employing it would baffle most of the rest of the world. Australians, in particular, would be puzzled. For us, the closer we are, the more casual we become. It's 'mate' here and 'mate' there, and an intense desire to act dumb, a fear that our friends might perceive us to be bunging something on, putting on side, if we speak any differently. How cultures vary. It's obvious that one of the national traits these men pride is blatant courtesy, doing what is seen to be polite. It reminds me of the young blokes in the bus shelter the other day as I crossed the broad rue La Fayette. You've dropped your glove, they shouted. And I had.

The men alongside have ordered scallops, and they pay particular attention to the texture, which is springy — *comme il faut* (as it should be), says the one in the cord blazer. His companion says he's going to Australia for the first time

in a couple of months. It wouldn't normally attract him, he
says, but he has friends living briefly in Sydney. You know, he
says, leaning forward across the table, I understand
Australians are quite casual. They have a '*minable mentalité*'
(this can best be translated as a 'lamentable' or 'pitiable'
culture). Yes, says his friend, Australians are a little backward.
Of course, they would have to be, he continues. They are
descended from the dregs of the British — convicts — and it
must rub off on the young. These men are not being nasty, let
me add quickly. They're just two decent blokes discussing
what they've gathered over the years about a place visited by
few of their compatriots older than thirty. I feel like
enlightening them a little but keep my powder dry.

A huge pear poached in beaujolais is as maroon as the
floor's tiles. Moreover, it's wonderfully tasty — and coloured
— all the way through. It's in a rich and equally dark syrup
with five croutons of brioche. The lake of syrup obscures a
creamy custard.

At the end of a fine lunch at a reasonable price I need
back-up. I divert the manager as he passes, repeating details
about the book I'm writing and that I've been here, there and
everywhere over the past dozen days and some places have
been very good and some have disappointed but today was
good and offered value for money in a place like Paris and it
would even cut it in my home town of Melbourne where the
middle-level restaurants are excellent for what you pay and
Aux Lyonnais could very well easily fit in among them and
what I need are the menu and wine list. I've turned into Molly
Bloom — the words tumble out and I must admit that I'm
pushing them at some volume so that the men alongside me
can't fail but overhear. They are, indeed, all ears.

I ask if Monsieur Ducasse ever visits the Lyonnais. Yes,
says the manager, he checks the bookings each day from
wherever he is in the world and calls in from time to time in
person. I pass the manager my card. He says he'd be

delighted to get me the lists and he retreats. Seconds pass. Then the bloke in the lemon Lacoste pullover who is about to visit Sydney leans forward and tells me he couldn't help hearing. Could I provide some restaurant recommendations for his visit? Hmmm, I reply, I don't know Sydney as well as I used to. And it's got nothing to do with Australia any more — it belongs to the world, and its prices. You'll eat as badly there for a huge fee as you can in London or Paris. Don't go to the esteemed Icebergs at Bondi, for example, because you will be served basic tucker at outrageous prices. Whereas Melbourne, a paradise of gourmand gustation at reasonable cost, is unknown to the entire world. I'll be home in a couple of days, I continue, and I'll send him a list of twenty Melbourne restaurants worth his time and money. He'll have to go south.

His thanks is fulsome as I pass across my card. He says he tried the Australian embassy and other official outlets and found nothing about contemporary art exhibitions or permanent galleries, the things he wants to see in Australia. Don't even mention restaurants. Yes, I say, it's typical. Our official Australian tourist offices cringe. They believe they can't sell Australia's real trumps — such as music, art and food — but have to project a mostly false notion of relaxed provincial casualness and broad egalitarianism in one of the most heterogeneous of nations. They feel they'll sell Australia and Australians better if they tell the world we're dumb-arses.

For years, I tell the *messieurs*, I have been recommending to official bodies to begin promoting Australia for its restaurants. I get laughed at. They think *I'm* the fool. But they don't know. It would be easier for me to write a book about diverse fine eating in my home town, for instance, than in Paris — but who would want to read it? If you need corroboration for my views, I say, I'll give you some addresses of Parisians I know who have been overwhelmed by the quality and variety of Melbourne restaurants.

The *messieurs* are appreciative. They won't need corroboration. It's only after I leave Aux Lyonnais that I begin to realise the trowel with which I've laid it on so thick is heavy in my backpack.

---

I've promised to drink a *ballon de rouge* with my friend Maurice Bensoussan, a writer of excellent food histories, grandfather, and former head of a French photocopying firm's United States operations. I meet him at Willi's Wine Bar in the rue des Petits Champs. He's just finishing off a bitter-chocolate terrine. Although he lives on the outskirts of the city, he comes up to lunch in Paris most days, to look up old friends and have a yarn. He says we should have co-ordinated better — we could have both been at the Lyonnais. But it's not as if we haven't seen each other lately. Not so long ago we were at this very table, I remind Maurice, and we ate a fine turret of raw tuna dice impregnated with parsley and shallots, Lyonnais sausage on lentils, and nice bits of beef on green beans with a gluey peppery sauce.

Willi's has been the quintessential Parisian bistro and wine bar since it was set up by Mark Williamson in 1980 — quite a long run. Indeed, it's credited with bringing the 'concept' to the French capital. Its food prices are fair and the wine list is long. Mark Williamson himself, a lanky Englishman with a drawl and a droll manner, joins us. He's wearing a white shirt with buttoned-down collars, a dark tweed jacket and a scarlet tie with orange buttercups. Maurice and I feel underdressed, I say. 'Ah, but you're relaxing,' says Mark. He's at work. He's come from his relatively new restaurant Macéo, just down the road. The name Willi, he tells me, by the way, is coincidental and has nothing to do with him — the bistro was named after Colette's husband.

Shop-talk dominates — as it must — and we bemoan the lack of adventure in Parisian eating-out. Its sameness.

Even its tradition. Critics are unable, apparently, to lever any changes for the better. In a city that is supposed to lead in many fields, the towel appears to have been thrown in. Even Senderens disclaiming high dining. Yes, I say, and the list at his new place reads like something from Melbourne ten years ago. For all that, I add, France seems to be changing slightly, accepting new ingredients and techniques, slowly recognising the New World contributions of diversifying raw materials and culinary techniques, and understanding that ordinary people want to eat out differently from in the fine-dine days.

Appreciating the best of French restaurant cooking is, it strikes me, a bit like being a fan of old cars. You can love DS Citroëns, for instance, for the style, mechanical refinement and elegance they had during the twenty years from 1955 in which they were produced. But even the best remaining examples of the model don't perform like contemporary saloons. These days it's all about performance. And French chefs are being outperformed.

There's a sigh or two and a few ums and ahs — no disagreement, if you like. I tell Maurice and Mark about my Fogón experience. Maurice hasn't been there, but Mark has, and was underwhelmed. He's glad I'll be so frank when I write about it. French critics aren't. He lists for me four restaurants worth trying, as he gets up to return to Macéo. They'll have to wait for my next trip.

A half-hour later Maurice and I are out the door, too. He wants to guide me to the closest Métro station but I insist on walking. He has to catch a train back south. A propos of nothing, I ask his views on the riots — on race relations in France in general. He'll admit that times are tough for many French of Arab descent, but he finds it hard to understand manifestations of racist behaviour, be they by French from Europe or Africa, north or south. When he was growing up, a Jew in Cairo, there was simply no question of not getting along with others in that very cosmopolitan city. It didn't enter his mind to exclude Arabs from friendship, he says.

I'm walking home up the rue Turgot, which gets a little steep as it approaches the place d'Anvers, where I know there's a market today. I'm having Maggie Wheels to dinner, and I shall do as the French do — see what's for sale, take it home and cook it.

A few paces ahead of me on the narrow pavement, a tall young fellow wrapped in a charcoal-grey overcoat ambles in the same direction. He's absorbed in a mobile-phone conversation. He has long dark hair and his head is inclined towards the phone, jamming it between his ear and his collarbone. Perhaps ten paces ahead of him, a frail old man on a stick suddenly emerges from his front door. As the young man draws level, the old man puts out a hand, rises up on tip-toe and whispers gruffly. I catch the last syllables — 'PTT'. As I pass, the young man makes a teapot handle with his right arm, the old man locks his left into it, and they begin a dodder up the footpath. The young man continues his phone conversation. I can see that from time to time he smiles and chortles. Seconds later I'm passing a post office — a 'PTT' in local parlance. They're almost halfway there.

And Maggie Wheels shall dine on rabbit *rillettes*, bream, sweated leeks and a camembert that the *fromagière* assures me is perfect for tonight. And we will wash them down with a new beaujolais, even though it's not the best of years.

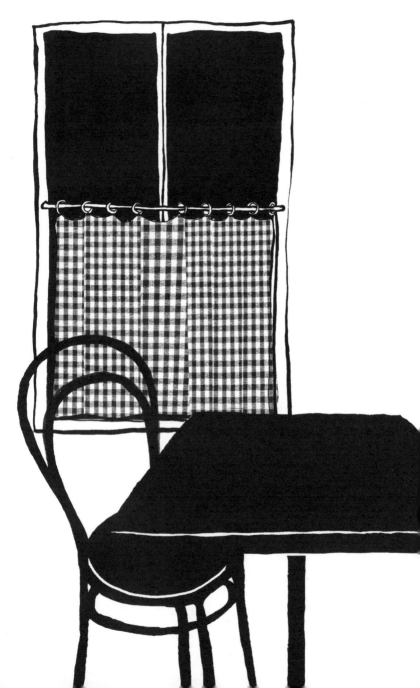

# acknowledgements

My thanks, yet again, go to the entire team at Murdoch Books, led by chief executive Juliet Rogers and publishing director Kay Scarlett. Editor Jane Price showed great feel for my words and made subtle and important improvements to them. Sarah Odgers and Antonia Pesenti created a design and illustrations perfectly in tune with my manuscript.

In Paris itself, I am indebted to the unstinting generosity of Pascal Barbot and Christophe Rohat at Astrance, Christian Le Squer and Patrick Simiand at Ledoyen and Jean-Claude Vrinat at Taillevent. Similarly, my thanks go to Eric Lanuit at the Lido and Christophe Millant at the Crazy Horse. Finally, I must thank family and friends who supported my gastronomic trek, gave important advice, and made the project so enjoyable: my wife Dominique, niece Magali Delouche, her parents Jean-Pierre and Josiane Delouche, and my dear friend Maurice Bensoussan.

First published in 2006 by Pier 9,
an imprint of Murdoch Books Pty Limited

Murdoch Books Australia
Pier 8/9, 23 Hickson Road, Millers Point NSW 2000
Phone : +61 (0) 2 8220 2000  Fax : +61 (0) 2 8220 2558

Murdoch Books UK Limited
Erico House, 6th Floor North, 93–99 Upper Richmond Road,
Putney, London SW15 2TG
Phone : +44 (0) 20 8785 5995  Fax : +44 (0) 20 8785 5985

Chief Executive: Juliet Rogers
Publishing Director: Kay Scarlett

Design manager: Vivien Valk
Design concept and designer: Sarah Odgers
Editor: Jane Price
Project Manager: Jacqueline Blanchard
Production: Monika Paratore

National Library of Australia Cataloguing-in-Publication Data
Downes, Stephen (Stephen L.).  Paris on a plate: a gastronomic diary.
ISBN 9781740458818.
ISBN 1 74045 881 8.
1. Downes, Stephen (Stephen L.) — Diaries.  2. Gastronomy.
3. Cookery, French.  4. Paris (France) — Description and travel.
I. Title. 641.013094436

Printed by Midas Printing (Asia) Ltd. in 2006. PRINTED IN CHINA.